ASIA BOND MONITOR
MARCH 2022

ASIAN DEVELOPMENT BANK

 Creative Commons Attribution 3.0 IGO license (CC BY 3.0 IGO)

Note:
ADB recognizes "China" as the People's Republic of China; "Hong Kong" and "Hongkong" as Hong Kong, China;
"Korea" as the Republic of Korea; "Russia" as the Russian Federation; "Siam" as Thailand; "Vietnam" as Viet Nam;
"Hanoi" as Ha Noi; and "Saigon" as Ho Chi Minh City.

Cover design by Erickson Mercado.

Contents

Emerging East Asian Local Currency
Bond Markets: A Regional Update

Emerging East Asian Local Currency Bond Markets: A Regional Update

Executive Summary

Recent Trends in Financial Conditions in Emerging East Asia

Monetary stances in emerging East Asia remain largely accommodative.[1] While the improving economic performance and rising inflation in advanced economies has led to adjustments in their monetary policies, most central banks in emerging East Asia maintained accommodative monetary policies, even as some regional markets, such as the Republic of Korea and Singapore, tightened their monetary stances due to inflationary pressure.

Ample liquidity supported regional financial conditions during the review period from 30 November 2021 to 9 March 2022, with some weakening signs related to the United States (US) Federal Reserve's tapering and its signaling of monetary tightening, and the Russian Federation's (Russia) invasion of Ukraine. Between 30 November 2021 and 9 March 2022, bond yields in emerging East Asia rose on inflationary pressure and spillovers from higher bond yields in major advanced markets. The majority of regional currencies depreciated against the US dollar, with most currencies posting relatively small exchange rate movements. Net portfolio inflows were recorded in the region, while equity markets continued to gain, particularly the markets of Association of Southeast Asian Nations (ASEAN) members on improved economic performance in the fourth quarter (Q4) of 2021. At the same time, risk premiums edged up due to increased risk aversion generated by subdued investment sentiment over the Federal Reserve's expected tightening and the Russian invasion of Ukraine.

The risk outlook for regional financial conditions is tilted to the downside. With progress in economic growth and persistent inflationary pressure in the US, the Federal Reserve started another round of rate hikes in 2022, bringing uncertainty to global liquidity conditions. The Russian invasion of Ukraine may further push up inflation via higher oil and food prices. Continued inflationary pressure could induce regional central banks to tighten, which in turn could affect liquidity and financial conditions. Other uncertainties include persistent supply chain disruptions and the future trajectory of the coronavirus disease (COVID-19) pandemic.

Recent Developments in Local Currency Bond Markets in Emerging East Asia

The size of the local currency (LCY) bond market in emerging East Asia climbed to USD22.8 trillion at the end of December 2021, following USD2.4 trillion of issuance in Q4 2021. LCY bond issuance in emerging East Asia for full-year 2021 reached USD9.0 trillion, expanding 7.1% y-o-y from USD8.4 billion in 2020 and marking the region's largest annual issuance total ever. ASEAN member economies recorded aggregate issuance of USD1.5 trillion in 2021, accounting for 17.0% of the region's annual total, up from a share of 14.7% in 2020. ASEAN issuance in 2021 also marked an annual record-high.

Government bonds accounted for 62.7% of LCY bonds outstanding in emerging East Asia at the end of December. The region's LCY government bond market expanded to a size of USD14.3 trillion in Q4 2021 on new issuance of USD1.3 trillion, which accounted for 56.7% of the region's total issuance during the quarter. ASEAN markets accounted for 10.0% of the region's outstanding government bonds at the end of 2021 and 29% of regional LCY government bond issuance in Q4 2021. Outstanding corporate bonds in emerging East Asia totaled USD8.5 trillion at the end of December, expanding at a pace of 2.8% q-o-q and 11.0% y-o-y in Q4 2021 amid economic recovery.

The maturity structure of emerging East Asia's LCY government bond markets continued to be concentrated in medium- to longer-term tenors. At the end of December, 53.8% of outstanding LCY government bonds in the region had a tenor of more than 5 years.

---

[1] Emerging East Asia comprises the People's Republic of China; Hong Kong, China; Indonesia; the Republic of Korea; Malaysia; the Philippines; Singapore; Thailand; and Viet Nam.

In terms of investor profile, financial institutions such as banks, pension funds, insurance companies, and mutual funds played an increasingly important role in regional LCY government bond markets in 2021, especially in Indonesia.

ASEAN+3's sustainable bond market saw rapid expansion in 2021.[2] In full-year 2021, ASEAN+3's total issuance of sustainable bonds rose to USD239.5 billion, more than doubling 2020's issuance of USD96.1 billion. Sustainable bonds outstanding reached USD430.7 billion at the end of December, with total issuance in Q4 2021 of USD58.0 billion.

Special Topics on Local Currency Bond Markets in Emerging East Asia

The *Asia Bond Monitor March 2022* issue features four special boxes and the results of the 2021 *AsianBondsOnline* Annual Bond Market Liquidity Survey.

Bond Market Special Boxes

Foreign Participation in Asian Local Currency Bond Markets and Financial Stability Risks

The development of LCY bond markets in emerging Asian economies has helped mitigate the negative impacts of currency and maturity mismatches. However, the expanding presence of foreign investors in these markets can amplify the risk of capital flow reversals during periods of heightened financial tension. A recent paper by Beirne, Renzhi, and Volz (2021) found that less-developed LCY bond markets are more susceptible to capital flow volatility due to foreign investor participation than more developed LCY bond markets. While foreign participation in LCY bond markets provides important risk-sharing and diversification benefits, authorities should be cautious of the potential financial stability risks to domestic markets.

Determinants of Sovereign Local Currency Bond Issuance in Emerging Markets

A recent study by Zheng et al. (2021) analyzed the determinants of sovereign LCY bond issuance in emerging markets and reported the following key findings. First, emerging market sovereign borrowers were more likely to issue LCY bonds amid a period of domestic currency appreciation before, but not after, the global financial crisis (GFC). Second, inflation-targeting governments tended to issue LCY debt before, but not after, the GFC, reflecting fading global concerns about inflation in the post-GFC period. Third, emerging market sovereign issuers that offered higher yields after the GFC were more likely to issue LCY bonds. The results suggest that return-seeking in the aftermath of the GFC allowed sovereign borrowers, including those with less robust fundamentals, to issue LCY bonds, facilitated by low interest rates globally and offshore LCY bond issuances.

Pricing of Frequent Green Bond Issuances

This box compares the yield difference between frequent and infrequent issuers of green bonds. While there are advantages for issuers of and investors in green bonds, information asymmetry remains a key challenge in the green bond market. Funding costs can be reduced by addressing information asymmetry, via a clear taxonomy, information-enhancing mechanisms, and a novel aspect in the market—frequent issuance. The Oaxaca–Blinder decomposition shows an unexplained yield difference of 68 basis points between frequent and infrequent green bond issuers. Thus, frequent green bond issuers can enjoy a cost advantage due to greater information transparency and a stronger environmental commitment.

Progress toward Greater Efficiency and Integrity in Sustainable Financial Markets: Summary of the Asian Development Bank–State Street Global Advisors Webinar Series

This box summarizes key points from discussions among a broad range of sustainable financial market stakeholders—including investors, regulators, and corporates—at a webinar series jointly hosted by the Asian Development Bank and State Street Global Advisors in November 2021. It was recognized that green investing represents a unique opportunity as demand for green investments rise. Investment managers are increasingly following environmental, social, and governance (ESG) principles, while corporates reported that enhanced disclosure improves ESG awareness and positively impacts investor preferences. Challenges remain in the sustainable market that can be addressed via standardized data and reporting, improved disclosure, and the development of ESG databases.

---

[2] For the discussion on sustainable bonds, ASEAN+3 includes ASEAN members Indonesia, Malaysia, the Philippines, Singapore, Thailand, and Viet Nam plus the People's Republic of China; Hong Kong, China; Japan; and the Republic of Korea.

Annual *AsianBondsOnline* Bond Market Liquidity Survey

Overall liquidity conditions in emerging East Asia's bond market improved slightly in 2021 compared with 2020, with 50% of survey respondents observing increased liquidity and narrowed bid–ask spreads for both government and corporate bonds. Over 70% of survey participants cited market sentiment as the most important factor affecting bond market liquidity in 2021, with a few other factors also cited as important such as domestic monetary policy, the lingering COVID-19 pandemic, and US monetary policy. On structural market development issues, hedging instruments remain the persistently least-developed factor that affects market liquidity, shedding light on the direction of future market developments.

Global and Regional Market Developments

Higher bond yields in advanced economies spilled over to emerging East Asia

Yields on 2-year and 10-year local currency (LCY) government bonds rose in advanced markets and most emerging East Asian markets between 30 November 2021 and 9 March 2022.[1] Robust economic recovery, rising inflation, and a shift in monetary policy stances in advanced economies have driven up bond yields in advanced markets. Higher bond yields in advanced economies and continued inflationary pressure from rising oil and food prices pushed up bond yields in emerging East Asia. While most regional central banks are maintaining accommodative monetary stances, widely anticipated monetary tightening by the Federal Reserve and the Russian invasion of Ukraine have heightened risk aversion and pushed up risk premiums. Regional financial conditions, while still robust, slightly weakened, as the majority of currencies depreciated and the strong performance momentum in equity markets softened during the review period (**Table A**).

In major advanced markets, progress in economic recovery and persistent inflation has led to expected monetary tightening and pushed up bond yields. In the US, 2-year and 10-year bond yields rose strongly by 111 basis points (bps) and 51 bps, respectively, between 30 November 2021 and 9 March 2022. The Federal Reserve announced at its 2–3 November meeting that it would taper its monthly purchases of Treasury assets by USD10 billion and mortgage-backed securities by USD5 billion. At its 14–15 December meeting, the Federal Reserve indicated that it would accelerate tapering by reducing Treasury purchases by USD20 billion and mortgage-backed securities by USD10 billion per month, aiming to end all asset purchases by March 2022.

Table A: Changes in Global Financial Conditions

	2-Year Government Bond (bps)	10-Year Government Bond (bps)	5-Year Credit Default Swap Spread (bps)	Equity Index (%)	FX Rate (%)
Major Advanced Economies					
United States	111	51	–	(6.3)	–
United Kingdom	93	72	6	1.9	(0.9)
Japan	9	11	0.3	(8.5)	(2.3)
Germany	25	57	8	(8.3)	(2.3)
Emerging East Asia					
China, People's Rep. of	(24)	(0.3)	2	(8.6)	0.7
Hong Kong, China	62	20	–	(12.1)	(0.3)
Indonesia	36	68	23	5.1	(0.1)
Korea, Rep. of	34	51	11	(7.6)	(3.8)
Malaysia	7	15	14	3.2	0.4
Philippines	44	41	30	(2.9)	(3.6)
Singapore	46	16	–	5.1	0.5
Thailand	(13)	29	9	4.8	2.2
Viet Nam	88	27	28	(0.3)	(0.5)

( ) = negative, – = not available, bps = basis points, FX = foreign exchange.
Notes:
1. Data reflect changes between 30 November 2021 and 9 March 2022.
2. A positive (negative) value for the FX rate indicates the appreciation (depreciation) of the local currency against the United States dollar.
Source: *AsianBondsOnline* computations based on Bloomberg LP data.

---

[1] Emerging East Asia comprises the People's Republic of China; Hong Kong, China; Indonesia; the Republic of Korea; Malaysia; the Philippines; Singapore; Thailand; and Viet Nam.

In its December projections, the Federal Reserve revised upward its 2022 forecasts for gross domestic product (GDP) growth and Personal Consumption Expenditures inflation to 4.0% and 2.6%, respectively, from its September forecasts of 3.8% and 2.2%. Per the dot plot released after the December Federal Open Market Committee meeting, the federal funds rate was projected to rise by 75 bps in 2022.

During it's 25–26 January meeting, the Federal Reserve affirmed that its asset purchase program would end in March and acknowledged that high inflation, continued economic recovery, and a strong labor market warranted an increase in the federal funds target range "soon." Nonfarm payroll additions in February rose to 678,000 from 481,000 in January and 588,000 in December. The unemployment rate also declined to 3.8% in February, an improvement from 4.0% in January and 3.9% in December. The Federal Reserve raised the federal funds rate by 25 bps at its 15–16 March meeting. Projections indicate a total of 175 bps rate hike in 2022 and 2023.

Continued economic growth and mounting inflation also led to Asset Purchase Programme (APP) adjustments by the European Central Bank (ECB). The euro area's GDP expanded 4.6% year-on-year (y-o-y) in the fourth quarter of 2021, up from 4.0% y-o-y in the third quarter. During its 10 March meeting, the ECB noted the euro area's economic growth and rising inflation. The ECB updated its GDP forecasts for 2021, 2022, and 2023 to 5.4%, 3.7%, and 2.8%, respectively, compared with December forecasts of 5.1%, 4.2%, and 2.9%. The ECB also raised its inflation forecasts for 2021, 2022, and 2023 to 2.6%, 5.1%, and 2.1%, respectively, from 2.6%, 3.2%, and 1.8%. Similar to the Federal Reserve, the ECB announced that bond purchases under the Pandemic Emergency Purchase Programme would end in March. During its 16 December meeting, the ECB said that following the end of such purchases, the ECB will temporarily increase bond purchases under its conventional APP from the current monthly pace of EUR20 billion to EUR40 billion in the second quarter of 2022 and to EUR30 billion in the third quarter. However, uncertainty related to the Russian invasion of Ukraine might influence these adjustments. At its 10 March meeting, the ECB accelerated its tapering of the APP, announcing monthly net purchases amounting to EUR40 billion in April, EUR30 billion in May, and EUR20 billion in June. If the data support it, the ECB might conclude net purchases in the third quarter of 2022.

At its 18 January meeting, the Bank of Japan (BOJ) revised its 2022 GDP growth and inflation forecasts upward to 3.8% and 1.1%, respectively, from previous forecasts of 2.9% and 0.9% made in October. The BOJ's monetary policy was largely left unchanged, with the short-term policy rate target maintained at −0.1%; the 10-year Japan Government Bond yield target held at zero; and the current purchase of government bonds, corporate bonds, and commercial paper unchanged. The BOJ expects its policy rates to remain either at or below current levels, but affirmed that it would end monthly asset purchases of corporate bonds and commercial paper in March.

While most regional central banks maintained easy monetary stances amid modest inflation, the Bank of Korea and Monetary Authority of Singapore began tightening their respective monetary policies due to inflationary pressure. Many regional central banks also reduced their LCY bond purchases in 2021 as economic activities gradually recovered (**Figure A**). Tracking rising bond yields in major advanced markets and rising inflation in the region, 2-year and 10-year bond yields rose in almost all emerging East Asian markets between 30 November and 9 March (**Figure B**).

Indonesia and the Philippines witnessed relatively large increases in 10-year bond yields of 68 bps and 41 bps,

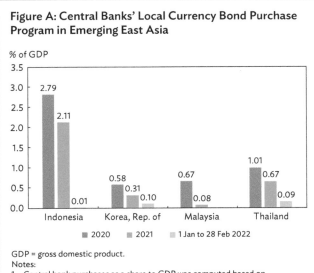

Figure A: Central Banks' Local Currency Bond Purchase Program in Emerging East Asia

% of GDP

■ 2020   ■ 2021   ■ 1 Jan to 28 Feb 2022

GDP = gross domestic product.
Notes:
1. Central bank purchases as a share to GDP was computed based on December 2021 GDP.
2. For Indonesia, data for 2022 cover the period 1 January to 18 February.
3. For Malaysia, data for 2022 cover the period 1 January to 31 January.
Sources: CEIC Data Company, Haver Analytics, and various local sources.

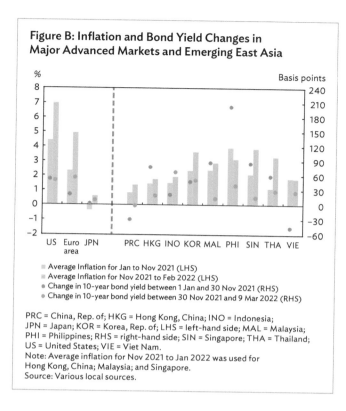

Figure B: Inflation and Bond Yield Changes in Major Advanced Markets and Emerging East Asia

- Average Inflation for Jan to Nov 2021 (LHS)
- Average Inflation for Nov 2021 to Feb 2022 (LHS)
- Change in 10-year bond yield between 1 Jan and 30 Nov 2021 (RHS)
- Change in 10-year bond yield between 30 Nov 2021 and 9 Mar 2022 (RHS)

PRC = China, Rep. of; HKG = Hong Kong, China; INO = Indonesia; JPN = Japan; KOR = Korea, Rep. of; LHS = left-hand side; MAL = Malaysia; PHI = Philippines; RHS = right-hand side; SIN = Singapore; THA = Thailand; US = United States; VIE = Viet Nam.
Note: Average inflation for Nov 2021 to Jan 2022 was used for Hong Kong, China; Malaysia; and Singapore.
Source: Various local sources.

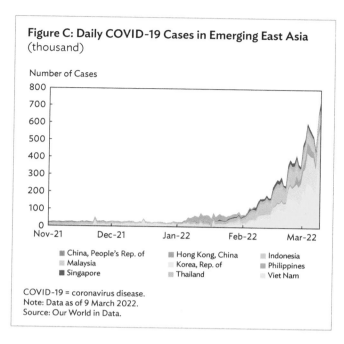

Figure C: Daily COVID-19 Cases in Emerging East Asia (thousand)

COVID-19 = coronavirus disease.
Note: Data as of 9 March 2022.
Source: Our World in Data.

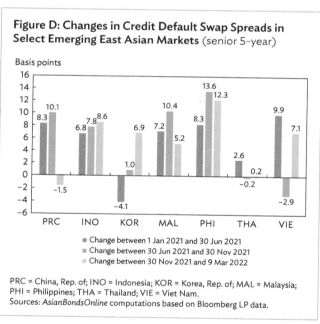

Figure D: Changes in Credit Default Swap Spreads in Select Emerging East Asian Markets (senior 5-year)

- Change between 1 Jan 2021 and 30 Jun 2021
- Change between 30 Jun 2021 and 30 Nov 2021
- Change between 30 Nov 2021 and 9 Mar 2022

PRC = China, Rep. of; INO = Indonesia; KOR = Korea, Rep. of; MAL = Malaysia; PHI = Philippines; THA = Thailand; VIE = Viet Nam.
Sources: AsianBondsOnline computations based on Bloomberg LP data.

respectively, amid subdued investment sentiment due to the Russian invasion of Ukraine, continued inflationary pressure, and the Federal Reserve's tapering and expected rate hikes. The Republic of Korea also recorded a large rise in 10-year bond yields of 51 bps, partly because the Bank of Korea continued raising its policy rate—by 25 bps on both 25 November 2021 and 14 January 2022. For short-term bonds, Viet Nam's 2-year yield recorded the largest rise in the region at 88 bps on increased financing demand and subdued investment sentiment given the rapid increase in local coronavirus disease (COVID-19) cases in February. This was followed by Hong Kong, China, where the 2-year yield jumped 62 bps during the review period amid rising local COVID-19 cases (**Figure C**).

The People's Republic of China (PRC) was the sole market in emerging East Asia that saw a decline in both its 2-year and 10-year bond yields. The decline in yields followed monetary easing by the People's Bank of China, which reduced the reserve requirement ratio by 50 bps on 6 December and further lowered the 1-year medium-term lending facility rate by 10 bps on 16 January in response to growth moderation. The PRC's GDP growth slowed to 4.0% y-o-y in the fourth quarter of 2021 from 4.9% y-o-y in the third quarter and 7.9% y-o-y in the second quarter. In December, the Asian Development Bank downgraded

its forecast for the PRC's GDP growth in full-year 2022 to 5.3% from 5.5% in September.

Strong economic recovery and expected monetary tightening in the US pushed up regional risk premiums in 2021. Risk premiums edged up further at the end of February following the Russian invasion of Ukraine (**Figure D**). Nevertheless, modest inflation and the gradual pace of recovery in emerging East Asia has allowed regional central banks to maintain their current

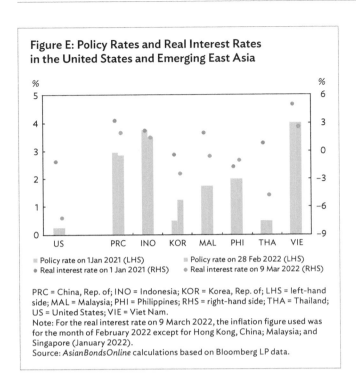

Figure E: Policy Rates and Real Interest Rates in the United States and Emerging East Asia

- Policy rate on 1 Jan 2021 (LHS)
- Policy rate on 28 Feb 2022 (LHS)
- Real interest rate on 1 Jan 2021 (RHS)
- Real interest rate on 9 Mar 2022 (RHS)

PRC = China, Rep. of; INO = Indonesia; KOR = Korea, Rep. of; LHS = left-hand side; MAL = Malaysia; PHI = Philippines; RHS = right-hand side; THA = Thailand; US = United States; VIE = Viet Nam.
Note: For the real interest rate on 9 March 2022, the inflation figure used was for the month of February 2022 except for Hong Kong, China; Malaysia; and Singapore (January 2022).
Source: AsianBondsOnline calculations based on Bloomberg LP data.

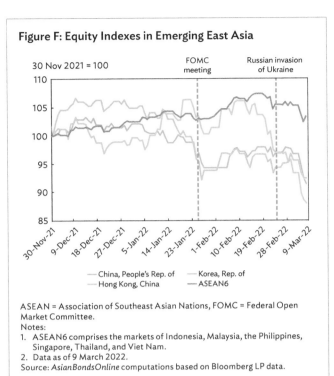

Figure F: Equity Indexes in Emerging East Asia

- China, People's Rep. of
- Hong Kong, China
- Korea, Rep. of
- ASEAN6

ASEAN = Association of Southeast Asian Nations, FOMC = Federal Open Market Committee.
Notes:
1. ASEAN6 comprises the markets of Indonesia, Malaysia, the Philippines, Singapore, Thailand, and Viet Nam.
2. Data as of 9 March 2022.
Source: AsianBondsOnline computations based on Bloomberg LP data.

accommodative monetary stances. Real interest rates remained relatively high in the region compared to the US and were positive in some regional markets (**Figure E**).

Negative sentiment generated by the Russian invasion of Ukraine on 24 February softened the bullish momentum in regional equity markets during the review period. The Association of Southeast Asian Nations (ASEAN) markets collectively rose, exhibiting a weighted average return of 3.3% between 30 November 2021 and 9 March 2022 on stronger GDP growth in the fourth quarter of 2021 compared to the previous quarter (**Figure F**). Hong Kong, China witnessed the region's largest retreat, with its equity market contracting 12.1% on soured investment sentiment over the Russian invasion of Ukraine as well as the rapid climb of local COVID-19 cases in February. A collective decline among regional equity markets was observed around the Federal Reserve's meeting on 25–26 January amid widespread expectations of tightening, as well as immediately after 24 February when the Russian invasion of Ukraine started.

Solid economic fundamentals, relatively higher real interest rates, and modest inflation make ASEAN assets attractive to foreign investors. Foreign equity portfolio flows remained sound in ASEAN markets on stronger economic performances during the review period (**Figure G**). Net equity foreign portfolio flows into

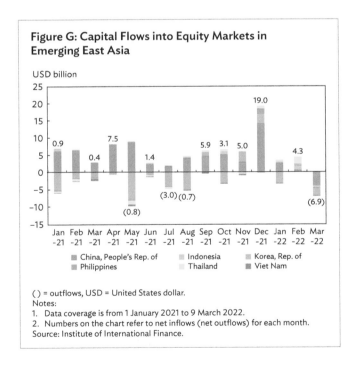

Figure G: Capital Flows into Equity Markets in Emerging East Asia

- China, People's Rep. of
- Philippines
- Indonesia
- Thailand
- Korea, Rep. of
- Viet Nam

( ) = outflows, USD = United States dollar.
Notes:
1. Data coverage is from 1 January 2021 to 9 March 2022.
2. Numbers on the chart refer to net inflows (net outflows) for each month.
Source: Institute of International Finance.

ASEAN markets recorded USD2.4 billion in December, reversing net outflows of USD0.9 billion in November. This was followed by net inflows of USD0.7 billion and USD3.3 billion in January and February, respectively. Thailand's equity market was the largest recipient of foreign capital flows in February, buoyed by optimism over its economic recovery due to the lifting of border restrictions effective 1 February. Its quarantine-free visa program for the fully vaccinated is expected to revive its tourism industry. Due to heightened risk aversion during the first 9 days of March following the Russian invasion of Ukraine, the PRC and the Republic of Korea witnessed outflows of USD4.1 billion and USD2.3 billion, respectively. Furthermore, the ASEAN markets experienced outflows of USD553.7 million.

Foreign portfolio flows to LCY bond markets in ASEAN remained robust through February 2022. Portfolio inflows in ASEAN bond markets reached USD1.6 billion and USD2.8 billion in December and January, respectively, led by Thailand (USD4.1billion) and Malaysia (USD2.5 billion), reversing average monthly outflows of USD1.3 billion from September to November (**Figure H**). In January, all regional markets except for Indonesia and the Philippines recorded inflows. ASEAN portfolio flows into the bond market further improved in February to USD3.6 billion from USD2.8 billion in the previous month.

Indonesia witnessed continuous foreign outflows from its bond market during most of 2021, partly driven by government efforts to promote domestic investment and stabilize capital flows.

As a result of positive inflows to most regional bond markets during the fourth quarter of 2021, the share of foreign holdings increased as of December (**Figure I**). Similar patterns can be observed in changes in the investor profiles of regional bond markets (**Figure J**). During 2021, the share of foreign holdings increased in the PRC, the Republic of Korea, and Malaysia, while it declined in Indonesia from 24.9% in January to 19.0% in December, as the government aimed to boost the domestic investor base in the bond market. Domestic financing institutions—particularly banks, insurance companies, and pension funds and mutual funds—now account for more than 50% of the domestic LCY bond market in Indonesia. Similar developments also occurred in the markets of Thailand and the Philippines. **Box 1** further discusses foreign participation in Asian LCY bond markets and financial stability risks.

During the review period, a majority of regional currencies posted small exchange rate movements of less than 1% versus the US dollar (**Figure K**). The best performing currency was the Thai baht on a strengthened domestic economy and outlook, rising 2.2% versus the US dollar. The Korean won and Philippine peso weakened the most, depreciating 3.8% and 3.6%, respectively.

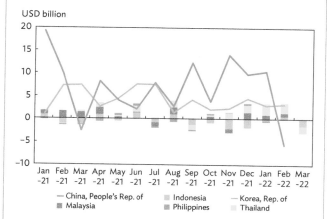

Figure H: Foreign Capital Flows in Local Currency Bond Markets in Emerging East Asia

USD = United States dollar.
Notes:
1. The Republic of Korea and Thailand provided data on bond flows. For the People's Republic of China, Indonesia, Malaysia, and the Philippines, month-on-month changes in foreign holdings of local currency government bonds were used as a proxy for bond flows.
2. Data are as of 9 March 2022 except for the People's Republic of China, the Republic of Korea, and Malaysia (28 February 2022); and the Philippines (31 January 2022).
3. Figures were computed based on 9 March 2022 exchange rates to avoid currency effects.
Sources: People's Republic of China (Bloomberg LP); Indonesia (Directorate General of Budget Financing and Risk Management, Ministry of Finance); Republic of Korea (Financial Supervisory Service); Malaysia (Bank Negara Malaysia); Philippines (Bureau of the Treasury); and Thailand (Thai Bond Market Association).

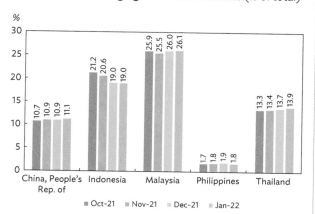

Figure I: Foreign Holdings of Local Currency Government Bonds in Select Emerging East Asian Markets (% of total)

Sources: People's Republic of China (Bloomberg LP and CEIC Data Company); Indonesia (Directorate General of Budget Financing and Risk Management, Ministry of Finance); Malaysia (Bank Negara Malaysia); Philippines (Bureau of the Treasury); and Thailand (Bank of Thailand).

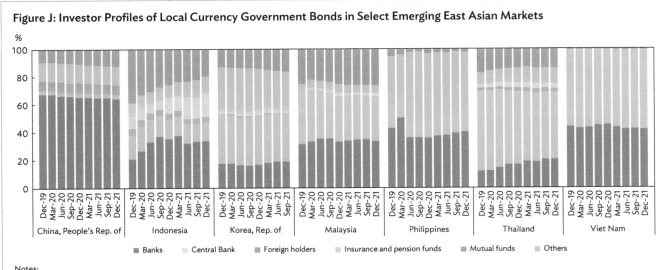

Figure J: Investor Profiles of Local Currency Government Bonds in Select Emerging East Asian Markets

Notes:
1. Data coverage is from December 2019 to December 2021 except for the Republic of Korea (September 2021).
2. "Others" include government institutions, individuals, securities companies, custodians, private corporations, and all other investors not elsewhere classified.
Source: *AsianBondsOnline* computations based on local market sources.

Box 1: Foreign Participation in Asian Local Currency Bond Markets and Financial Stability Risks

Local currency (LCY) bond markets have continued to develop in emerging Asian economies since the early 2000s, helping to mitigate against currency and maturity mismatches and reducing reliance on cross-border, bank-based finance.[a] LCY bond market development can also help reduce exposure to global shocks by reducing reliance on foreign currency borrowing. The share of foreign currency debt in emerging Asia, while still pervasive, has declined since 2000 as a result (**Figure B1.1**). Focusing on emerging Asian economies, this box examines the potential financial stability implications of foreign investor participation in LCY bond markets.

While the development of LCY bond markets has helped to reduce the currency mismatch issue in emerging Asian markets by facilitating borrowing abroad in the domestic currency, the increased presence of foreign investors in these markets can amplify the risk of capital flow reversals during periods of heightened financial tension. Excess capital flow volatility can also be related to the so-called "original sin redux," whereby unhedged foreign investors in LCY bond

markets are exposed to currency risks (Carstens and Shin 2019). In addition, while foreign investor participation in LCY bond markets can help lower bond yields, the volatility of yields tends to increase along with the foreign purchase of LCY bonds (e.g., Ebeke and Lu 2015). LCY bond markets also tend to be more susceptible to global financial shocks when foreign participation exceeds a given threshold, while the diversification benefits can be negatively affected by high exchange-rate volatility (Turner 2012). Foreign investors in LCY bond markets also tend to be more responsive than domestic investors to changes in global interest rates, which can amplify the exposure of LCY bond markets to foreign shocks.

A recent paper by Beirne, Renzhi, and Volz (2021) revisits this issue for a sample of 10 emerging Asian economies from 1999 to 2020. Drawing on structural panel vector autoregression techniques, they found that less-developed LCY bond markets are more susceptible to capital flow volatility due to foreign investor participation than those with more developed LCY bond markets (**Figure B1.2**).

---

[a] This box was written by John Beirne, research fellow at the Asian Development Bank Institute; Nuobu Renzhi, assistant professor at the Capital University of Economics and Business in the People's Republic of China; and Ulrich Volz, director of the Centre for Sustainable Finance at SOAS University of London and senior research fellow at the German Development Institute.

continued on next page

Box 1 *continued*

Figure B1.1: Foreign Currency Debt and Currency Mismatches in Emerging Asia

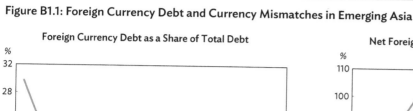

Notes: Emerging Asia comprises the People's Republic of China; Hong Kong, China; India; Indonesia; the Republic of Korea; Malaysia; the Philippines; Singapore; Thailand; and Viet Nam. The data are computed as gross-domestic-product-weighted averages for the 10 economies in the sample.
Sources: Authors' calculations based on data from the International Monetary Fund, Bank for International Settlements, Institute for International Finance, and China Economic Database.

Figure B1.2: Responses in Capital Flow Volatility to Shocks Imposed on Local Currency Bond Market Capitalization and Foreign Investor Participation in Local Currency Bond Markets

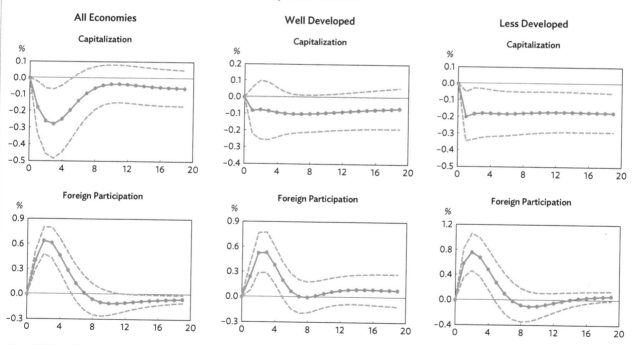

Notes: "Well developed" and "less developed" refer to economies with an average local currency bond market capitalization to gross domestic product ratio that is higher and lower, respectively, than the regional average over the period 1999–2020. Median responses with 95% confidence bands are shown as dashed lines. The vertical axes denote percentage points, while the horizontal axes refer to the number of months.
Source: Beirne, Renzhi, and Volz (2021).

continued on next page

Box 1   *continued*

Whereas positive LCY bond market capitalization shocks help to stabilize capital flows, as expected, the opposite effect is found for foreign investor participation shocks. Moreover, the sharp increase in capital flow volatility from these latter shocks is much more pronounced for less-developed LCY bond markets. Specifically, a positive shock to foreign investor participation of 1 percentage point yields a rise in capital flow volatility in less-developed markets by around 0.8 percentage points at peak. This compares to around 0.5 percentage points for well-developed markets. Therefore, while foreign participation in LCY bond markets provides important risk-sharing and diversification benefits for LCY bond markets, domestic markets should be cautious of the potential financial stability risks. Strengthening the local investor base should remain key, as well as developing further currency-hedging capabilities to enable foreign investors to manage currency risks.

References

Beirne, John, Nuobu Renzhi, and Ulrich Volz. 2021. "Local Currency Bond Markets, Foreign Investor Participation and Capital Flow Volatility in Emerging Asia." *Singapore Economic Review.* https://www.worldscientific.com/doi/10.1142/S0217590821410083 (published online 17 June 2021).

Carstens, Agustín, and Hyun Song Shin. 2019. "Emerging Markets Aren't Out of the Woods Yet." *Foreign Affairs.* https://www.foreignaffairs.com/articles/2019-03-15/emerging-markets-arent-out-woods-yet (published online 15 March 2019).

Ebeke, Christian, and Yinqiu Lu. 2015. "Emerging Market Local Currency Bond Yields and Foreign Holdings: A Fortune or Misfortune?" *Journal of International Money and Finance* 59 (C): 203–19. https://www.sciencedirect.com/science/article/pii/S0261560615001217.

Turner, Philip, 2012. "The Global Long Term Interest Rate, Financial Risks, and Policy Choices in EMEs." BIS Working Papers No. 441. Basel: Bank for International Settlements. https://www.bis.org/publ/work441.htm.

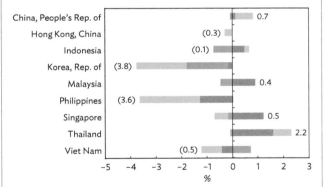

Figure K: Changes in Spot Exchange Rates versus the United States Dollar

China, People's Rep. of 0.7
Hong Kong, China (0.3)
Indonesia (0.1)
Korea, Rep. of (3.8)
Malaysia 0.4
Philippines (3.6)
Singapore 0.5
Thailand 2.2
Viet Nam (0.5)

■ 30 Nov to 31 Dec 2021   ■ 31 Dec 2021 to 31 Jan 2022   ■ 31 Jan to 9 Mar 2022

( ) = negative:
Notes:
1. Numbers on the chart refer to the net change for the three periods.
3. A positive (negative) value for the foreign exchange rate indicates the appreciation (depreciation) of the local currency against the United States dollar.
Source: *AsianBondsOnline* computations based on Bloomberg LP data.

Financial conditions in the region slightly weakened during the review period and the risk outlook to regional financial markets remains tilted toward the downside. Uncertainties include the fallout from the Russian invasion of Ukraine, expected tightening in US monetary policy, the trajectory of the COVID-19 pandemic, as well as continued inflationary pressure. **Box 2** shows evidence of the factors that drive sovereign LCY bond issuance in emerging markets.

Box 2: Determinants of Sovereign Local Currency Bond Issuance in Emerging Markets

In 2021, the aggregate size of local currency (LCY) bond markets in emerging East Asia reached 120% of the region's gross domestic product, of which more than 80% was in government bonds.[a] Emerging market LCY bond markets have grown rapidly since the global financial crisis (GFC). The governments of both advanced economies and emerging markets have expanded their borrowing since the GFC, when the United States (US) Federal Reserve forcefully cut interest rates to restore financial stability (**Figure B2**). The post-GFC, global low-interest-rate environment, which reduced the cost of borrowing, contributed to the growth of borrowing.

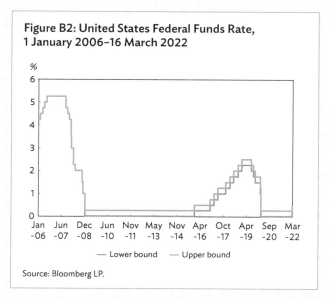

Figure B2: United States Federal Funds Rate, 1 January 2006–16 March 2022

Source: Bloomberg LP.

In the late 1990s and 2000s, many emerging markets adopted managed exchange rate flexibility, inflation-targeting policies, precautionary management of international reserves, and macroprudential policies. Since the GFC, a sharp drop in the yields on US bonds encouraged a global search for returns, thereby reducing the sovereign spreads of most emerging markets to single digits. Consequently, the institutional investors of advanced economies began to invest in the LCY bonds of many emerging markets, allowing them to borrow abroad in both foreign and domestic currencies. This was a game changer since emerging markets were traditionally unable to borrow abroad in their domestic currencies, a phenomenon known in economics as the "original sin."

A natural question that arises is when do emerging market governments choose to issue bonds in domestic currency rather than foreign currency? Zheng et al. (2021) empirically examine this issue, using 1970–2018 sovereign bond issuance data from the Thomson Reuters Eikon database. Their data cover eight major emerging market sovereign borrowers: Brazil, the People's Republic of China, India, Indonesia, Mexico, the Russian Federation, South Africa, and Turkey. Their analysis yields three main findings.

First, emerging market sovereign borrowers are more likely to issue LCY bonds when the domestic currency appreciates, but this only held before the GFC. Currency appreciation increases the prospective returns on LCY-denominated assets, which then increases investor demand. However, the association between currency appreciation and investor demand weakened after the GFC. One possible explanation is that issuers found it more attractive to borrow in US dollars because they expected the US low-interest-rate environment to persist for a long time.

Second, inflation-targeting economies tended to issue LCY bonds before but not after the GFC. These economies generally have more credible monetary policies and are less likely to inflate away their public debt burden. The insignificant role of inflation targeting after the GFC reflects fading global concerns about inflation.

Third, emerging markets that have offered higher sovereign yields since the GFC are more likely to issue LCY-denominated bonds. This finding is consistent with the global search for returns after the Federal Reserve cut interest rates to almost zero.

The evidence suggests that the search for yield by investors in advanced economies in the post-GFC period has made it possible for even emerging markets with less robust fundamentals to issue sovereign LCY bonds. Furthermore, the coronavirus disease (COVID-19) crisis is likely to significantly increase the borrowing requirements of emerging market governments. Therefore, potential sovereign overborrowing, facilitated by the post-COVID-19 global low-interest-rate environment and the ability to borrow abroad in one's domestic currency, poses a risk to the financial stability of emerging markets.

[a] This box is based on Zheng, Huanhuan, Joshua Aizenman, Yothin Jinjarak, and Donghyun Park. 2021. "Good-Bye Original Sin, Hello Risk On-Off, Financial Fragility, and Crises? *Journal of International Money and Finance*" 117 (2021): 1024–42; *AsianBondsOnline*. Data Portal. https://asianbondsonline.adb.org/data-portal/ (accessed October 29, 2021).

Bond Market Developments in the Fourth Quarter of 2021

Size and Composition

Emerging East Asia's bond market reached a size of USD22.8 trillion at the end of December 2021.

The amount of outstanding local currency (LCY) bonds in emerging East Asia continued to expand in the fourth quarter (Q4) of 2021, amounting to USD22.8 trillion at the end of December.[2] The overall growth of 3.6% quarter-on-quarter (q-o-q) in Q4 2021 was the same as that of the third quarter (Q3), as the pace of growth in both the government and corporate bond segments was little changed between the 2 quarters. The decline in q-o-q growth in five of region's nine markets between Q3 2021 and Q4 2021 was offset by steady bond market growth in the People's Republic of China (PRC) combined with faster growth in Hong Kong, China; Indonesia; and Viet Nam (**Figure 1a**).

All nine markets in emerging East Asia posted positive q-o-q growth rates in Q4 2021, with Viet Nam; Indonesia; and Hong Kong, China posting the fastest expansions. Meanwhile, Thailand, Malaysia, and the Philippines recorded the slowest q-o-q growth rates in Q4 2021.

On a year-on-year (y-o-y) basis, overall growth in emerging East Asia's LCY bond market picked up, rising to 12.8% in Q4 2021 from 12.3% in Q3 2021 (**Figure 1b**). Five of the region's nine markets posted higher y-o-y growth rates in Q4 2021 than in the previous quarter. The LCY bond markets in Viet Nam, Singapore, and Indonesia recorded the region's fastest y-o-y expansions, while those of the Republic of Korea; Thailand; and Hong Kong, China experienced the weakest growth in Q4 2021. Nonetheless, all nine regional markets recorded positive y-o-y growth during the quarter.

The LCY bond market in the PRC remained the region's largest, with an outstanding bond stock amounting to USD18.1 trillion at the end of December. The PRC's

Figure 1a: Growth of Local Currency Bond Markets in the Third and Fourth Quarters of 2021 (q-o-q, %)

q-o-q = quarter-on-quarter, Q3 = third quarter, Q4 = fourth quarter.
Notes:
1. For Singapore, corporate bonds outstanding are based on *AsianBondsOnline* estimates.
2. Growth rates are calculated from local currency base and do not include currency effects.
3. Emerging East Asia growth figures are based on 31 December 2021 currency exchange rates and do not include currency effects.
Sources: People's Republic of China (CEIC Data Company); Hong Kong, China (Hong Kong Monetary Authority); Indonesia (Bank Indonesia; Directorate General of Budget Financing and Risk Management, Ministry of Finance; and Indonesia Stock Exchange); Republic of Korea (KG Zeroin Corporation and The Bank of Korea); Malaysia (Bank Negara Malaysia); Philippines (Bureau of the Treasury and Bloomberg LP); Singapore (Monetary Authority of Singapore, Singapore Government Securities, and Bloomberg LP); Thailand (Bank of Thailand); and Viet Nam (Bloomberg LP and Vietnam Bond Market Association).

share of the region's total bond market rose to 79.5% in Q4 2021 from 79.2% in the prior quarter. Overall growth was steady at 3.9% q-o-q between Q3 2021 and Q4 2021. The uptick in the growth of government bonds from 4.1% q-o-q in Q3 2021 to 4.5% q-o-q in Q4 2021 offset the slowdown in the growth of corporate bonds from 3.7% q-o-q in Q3 2021 to 2.9% q-o-q in Q4 2021. Growth in the government bond segment was supported by the strong expansion of outstanding local government bonds and Treasury and other government bonds, as the government continued debt issuance to support economic recovery. Meanwhile, rising default risk in property bonds dampened market sentiment, leading to a drop in issuance and weaker growth in the outstanding corporate bond stock in Q4 2021 compared to the prior quarter. On a y-o-y basis, growth in the PRC's LCY bond market rose to 13.6% in Q4 2021 from 12.8% in Q3 2021.

---

[2] Emerging East Asia comprises the People's Republic of China; Hong Kong, China; Indonesia; the Republic of Korea; Malaysia; the Philippines; Singapore; Thailand; and Viet Nam.

Figure 1b: Growth of Local Currency Bond Markets in the Third and Fourth Quarters of 2021 (y-o-y, %)

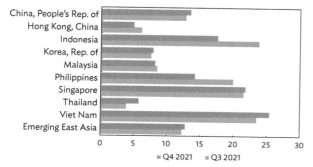

Q3 = third quarter, Q4 = fourth quarter, y-o-y = year-on-year.
Notes:
1. For Singapore, corporate bonds outstanding are based on *AsianBondsOnline* estimates.
2. Growth rates are calculated from local currency base and do not include currency effects.
3. Emerging East Asia growth figures are based on 31 December 2021 currency exchange rates and do not include currency effects.
Sources: People's Republic of China (CEIC Data Company); Hong Kong, China (Hong Kong Monetary Authority); Indonesia (Bank Indonesia; Directorate General of Budget Financing and Risk Management, Ministry of Finance; and Indonesia Stock Exchange); Republic of Korea (KG Zeroin Corporation and The Bank of Korea); Malaysia (Bank Negara Malaysia); Philippines (Bureau of the Treasury and Bloomberg LP); Singapore (Monetary Authority of Singapore, Singapore Government Securities, and Bloomberg LP); Thailand (Bank of Thailand); and Viet Nam (Bloomberg LP and Vietnam Bond Market Association).

The Republic of Korea's LCY bond market reached a size of USD2.4 trillion at the end of December, thus maintaining its position as the region's second-largest LCY bond market. However, its share of the regional LCY bond stock dipped to 10.5% in Q4 2021 from 10.7% in Q3 2021. Overall growth slipped to 1.5% q-o-q in Q4 2021 from 1.6% in the previous quarter. Growth in the government bond segment dropped to 0.2% q-o-q in Q4 2021 from 1.9% q-o-q in the previous quarter. Outstanding central government bonds continued to contract, dropping 7.1% q-o-q in Q4 2021 after declining 2.1% q-o-q in Q3 2021, as the government continued to wind down debt issuance. Growth in the corporate bond segment rose to 2.4% q-o-q in Q4 2021 from 1.4% q-o-q in Q3 2021, buoyed by a rebound in issuance amid robust economic recovery. On an annual basis, the Republic of Korea's LCY bond market expanded 7.9% y-o-y in Q4 2021, up from 7.6% y-o-y in the previous quarter.

The outstanding LCY bond stock in Hong Kong, China amounted to USD323.9 billion at the end of December 2021. Overall growth jumped to 4.0% q-o-q in Q4 2021 from 0.1% q-o-q in Q3 2021, underpinned by a faster

growth in the government bond segment and a rebound in the corporate bond segment. Government bonds outstanding expanded 5.2% q-o-q in Q4 2021, up from 3.0% q-o-q in the previous quarter. To meet strong market demand amid ample liquidity in the financial system, the Hong Kong Monetary Authority increased its issuance of Exchange Fund Bills (EFBs) in Q4 2021, thus contributing to the growth of outstanding government bond stock. Corporate bonds outstanding rose 2.7% q-o-q in Q4 2021, reversing the 2.9% q-o-q contraction Q3 2021, as initial signs of economic recovery boosted investor confidence. On a y-o-y basis, the LCY bond market in Hong Kong, China expanded 5.0% in Q4 2021 versus 6.1% in Q3 2021.

The aggregate amount of LCY bonds outstanding among members of the Association of Southeast Asian Nations (ASEAN) reached USD2.0 trillion at the end of December, up from USD1.9 trillion at the end of September.[3] The ASEAN member economies' share of the region's total bond stock dipped to 8.6% in Q4 2021 from 8.7% in the previous quarter. The amount of LCY bonds outstanding in the markets of ASEAN member economies expanded 2.6% q-o-q and 13.6% y-o-y in Q4 2021, down from 3.8% q-o-q and 14.5% y-o-y in Q3 2021. At the end of December, ASEAN member economies' aggregate LCY government bond stock stood at USD1.4 trillion, accounting for a 72.6% share of the ASEAN total. The corporate bond stock was USD538.4 billion and accounted for the remaining 27.4% share. Singapore, Thailand, and Malaysia were home to the three largest LCY bond markets among ASEAN members at the end of December.

Singapore's LCY bond market reached a size of USD449.5 billion at the end of December. Overall growth dropped to 3.8% q-o-q in Q4 2021 from 6.4% q-o-q in the prior quarter, as a slowdown in the expansion of the government bond segment outpaced an uptick in the growth of the corporate bond segment. Growth in outstanding government bonds dropped to 4.1% q-o-q in Q4 2021 from 8.0% q-o-q in Q3 2021, mainly due to a contraction in outstanding Singapore Government Securities. Meanwhile, outstanding corporate bonds rose 3.3% q-o-q in Q4 2021, up from 3.0% q-o-q in the prior quarter. On an annual basis, Singapore's LCY bond market grew 21.9% y-o-y in Q4 2021 versus 21.6% y-o-y in Q3 2021.

---

[3] LCY bond statistics for ASEAN include the markets of Indonesia, Malaysia, the Philippines, Singapore, Thailand, and Viet Nam.

The stock of outstanding LCY bonds in Thailand stood at USD443.5 billion at the end of December. Overall growth declined to 1.1% q-o-q in Q4 2021 from 2.5% q-o-q in Q3 2021 as growth in both the government and corporate bond segments eased. Government bonds outstanding rose 1.6% q-o-q in Q4 2021, down from 2.2% q-o-q in the previous quarter mainly due to contractions in Bank of Thailand bonds and state-owned enterprise and other bonds, as well as weaker growth in government bonds and Treasury bills. Growth in outstanding corporate bonds plummeted to 0.01% q-o-q in Q4 2021 from 3.4% q-o-q in the previous quarter, due to maturities and a contraction in issuance amid lingering uncertainties over tourism and economic revival. On a y-o-y basis, Thailand's LCY bond market posted 5.8% growth in Q4 2021, up from 3.9% in the prior quarter.

Malaysia's LCY bond market expanded 1.0% q-o-q and 8.2% y-o-y to reach USD416.7 billion at the end of Q4 2021. However, growth eased from 1.5% q-o-q and 8.5% y-o-y in Q3 2021. Outstanding government bonds expanded 1.2% q-o-q in Q4 2021, down from a 1.5% q-o-q gain in Q3 2021. A contraction in issuance of Treasury and other government bonds, as well as lack of issuance of new central bank bills, contributed to the slowdown in growth of outstanding government bonds. Growth in corporate bonds outstanding also slipped to 0.8% q-o-q in Q4 2021 from 1.4% q-o-q in the previous quarter.

Malaysia's *sukuk* (Islamic bond) market continued to be the largest in emerging East Asia. At the end of December, total *sukuk* outstanding in Malaysia reached USD264.7 billion. Malaysia's government *sukuk* outstanding stood at USD110.2 billion, or 48.4% of the total LCY government bond market in Q4 2021. With an outstanding amount of USD154.4 billion, corporate *sukuk* dominated Malaysia's corporate bond market with an 81.8% share of the total.

LCY bonds outstanding in Indonesia reached USD372.6 billion at the end of December. Overall growth rose to 4.4% q-o-q in Q4 2021 from 3.6% q-o-q in Q3 2021 due to faster growth in the government bond segment combined with a rebound in the corporate bond segment. The stock of LCY government bonds increased 4.6% q-o-q in Q4 2021 versus 4.0% q-o-q in the prior quarter. Growth in the government bond segment stemmed from expansions in central government and Bank Indonesia bonds, as nontradable bonds recorded

a contraction during the quarter. Corporate bonds outstanding rose 2.0% q-o-q in Q4 2021, reversing the 0.2% q-o-q contraction in the previous quarter, as issuance exceeded maturities. On a y-o-y basis, Indonesia's bond market posted growth of 17.7 % in Q4 2021, down from 23.9% in Q3 2021.

Indonesia's *sukuk* market amounted to USD68.0 billion at the end of December. Government *sukuk* stood at USD65.6 billion, representing 19.1% of Indonesia's LCY government bond market. Corporate *sukuk* totaled USD2.4 billion, or 8.1% of Indonesia's total LCY corporate bond market.

The Philippines LCY bond market totaled USD191.9 billion at the end of December. Overall growth dropped to 0.3% q-o-q in Q4 2021 from 4.4% q-o-q in Q3 2021. The growth slowdown was due to weaker growth in the government bond segment combined with a continuing contraction in the corporate bond segment. Outstanding government bonds were roughly unchanged, expanding 0.5% q-o-q in Q4 2021, down from a 6.2% q-o-q gain in the prior quarter as the government sought to manage its debt-to-gross-domestic-product (GDP) ratio. Treasury bonds were the sole driver of growth in Q4 2021, as the amount of outstanding Treasury bills, Bangko Sentral ng Pilipinas securities, and other bonds contracted. Due to maturities, corporate bonds outstanding declined 1.3% q-o-q in Q4 2021 after contracting 5.1% q-o-q in Q3 2021. On an annual basis, the stock of LCY bonds in the Philippines expanded 14.2% y-o-y in Q4 2021, down from 20.0% y-o-y in Q3 2021.

Viet Nam's LCY bond market remained both the smallest and the fastest-growing market in the region with bonds outstanding amounting to USD91.5 billion at the end of December. Overall growth accelerated to 9.8% q-o-q in Q4 2021 from 8.1% q-o-q in the previous quarter, driven by faster expansions in the government and corporate bond segments. Government bonds outstanding rose 5.3% q-o-q in Q4 2021, up from 4.2% q-o-q in the preceding quarter. The growth in government bonds was supported by a 5.7% q-o-q expansion in Treasury bonds and a 1.7% q-o-q rise in government-guaranteed and municipal bonds in Q4 2021; there were no outstanding central bank bills at the end of December. Corporate bonds outstanding jumped 22.7% q-o-q in Q4 2021, up from 21.4% q-o-q in the previous quarter, on the back of a resurgence in issuance. On a y-o-y basis, Viet Nam's outstanding LCY bond stock rose 25.5% in Q4 2021 versus 23.6% in Q3 2021.

Government bonds continued to comprise a majority of emerging East Asia's LCY bond market in Q4 2021. The region's government bond stock amounted to USD14.3 trillion in nominal terms, accounting for a 62.7% share of the total LCY bond market at the end of December (**Table 1**). Growth in the region's government bond market rose slightly to 4.0% q-o-q in Q4 2021 from 3.9% q-o-q in Q3 2021. All nine government bond markets in the region posted positive q-o-q growth rates in Q4 2021. Growth in the PRC's government bond market was broadly steady between Q3 2021 and Q4 2021, while Hong Kong, China; Indonesia; and Viet Nam experienced faster q-o-q growth in government bonds in Q4 2021 versus Q3 2021. The rest of the region's market recorded a slowdown in growth. On a y-o-y basis, emerging East Asia's government bond stock rose 13.9% in Q4 2021, up from 13.5% in the previous quarter.

The PRC and the Republic of Korea remained home to the two largest government bond markets in emerging East Asia with a combined share of 88.8% of the region's total government bond stock at the end of Q4 2021. ASEAN member economies accounted for a combined 10.0% of the region's total government bond market. The largest government bond markets among ASEAN member economies were those of Indonesia, Thailand, and Singapore.

The maturity profile of emerging East Asia's government bonds was mostly concentrated in medium- to longer-term bonds at the end of December (**Figure 2**). The exceptions were the PRC and Hong Kong, China, where short-term bonds comprised a relatively larger share of total outstanding bonds. In both cases, market demand was higher for shorter-dated bonds. On the other hand, longer-dated bonds with tenors of 10 years or longer dominated the markets of Viet Nam, Thailand, and the Republic of Korea.

LCY corporate bonds outstanding in emerging East Asia amounted to USD8.5 trillion at the end of December, representing 37.3% of the region's total LCY bond market. Growth in the region's LCY bond market eased to 2.8% q-o-q in Q4 2021 from 3.1% q-o-q in the previous quarter, driven primarily by a slowdown in the PRC market, the region's largest corporate bond market.

The corporate bond markets of the PRC and the Republic of Korea accounted for 91.8% of the region's total corporate bonds outstanding at the end of December. ASEAN member economies' share stood at 6.3%. Among ASEAN member economies, Malaysia, Singapore, and Thailand had the largest shares of corporate bonds outstanding, while Viet Nam remained home to the smallest corporate bond market in the region.

Emerging East Asia's total LCY bonds outstanding were equivalent to 98.6% of the region's GDP at the end of December, expanding from 97.5% in September and from 97.8% in December 2020 (**Table 2**). The higher share was largely due to governments continuing to mobilize debt financing for economic recovery and pandemic support programs, but GDP growth in the region was slowed by uncertainty due to episodes of surges in coronavirus disease (COVID-19) cases. The slowdown in the PRC's exceptionally large economy in Q4 2021 considerably contributed to the moderation of the region's aggregate GDP growth.

All economies in the region saw increases in their bond market share to GDP from Q3 2021 to Q4 2021 except for the Philippines, which posted a decline as a result of less borrowing during Q4 2021 and a better than expected quarterly GDP growth. The bond market-GDP-share exceeded 100% in the Republic of Korea, Malaysia, Singapore, and the PRC. Viet Nam's bond market as a share of GDP was the smallest in the region at the end of Q4 2021 at 24.9%.

Emerging East Asia's government bonds increased to the equivalent of 61.8% of the region's GDP in Q4 2021 from 60.8% in Q3 2021, while corporate bonds marginally increased to 36.8% of GDP from 36.7% over the same period. The regional market with the highest share of government bonds to GDP in Q4 2021 was Singapore (77.2%). For corporate bonds, it was the Republic of Korea (86.8%).

Table 1: Size and Composition of Local Currency Bond Markets

	Q4 2020 Amount (USD billion)	Q4 2020 % share	Q3 2021 Amount (USD billion)	Q3 2021 % share	Q4 2021 Amount (USD billion)	Q4 2021 % share	Growth Rate (LCY-base %) Q4 2020 q-o-q	Growth Rate (LCY-base %) Q4 2020 y-o-y	Growth Rate (LCY-base %) Q4 2021 q-o-q	Growth Rate (LCY-base %) Q4 2021 y-o-y	Growth Rate (USD-base %) Q4 2020 q-o-q	Growth Rate (USD-base %) Q4 2020 y-o-y	Growth Rate (USD-base %) Q4 2021 q-o-q	Growth Rate (USD-base %) Q4 2021 y-o-y
China, People's Rep. of														
Total	15,537	100.0	17,190	100.0	18,117	100.0	3.3	20.5	3.9	13.6	7.5	28.5	5.4	16.6
Government	9,978	64.2	11,043	64.2	11,701	64.6	3.8	20.6	4.5	14.2	8.0	28.7	6.0	17.3
Corporate	5,559	35.8	6,146	35.8	6,416	35.4	2.4	20.1	2.9	12.4	6.5	28.2	4.4	15.4
Hong Kong, China														
Total	310	100.0	312	100.0	324	100.0	5.1	6.1	4.0	5.0	5.1	6.6	3.8	4.4
Government	153	49.3	161	51.6	169	52.2	2.3	0.2	5.2	11.2	2.3	0.7	5.0	10.5
Corporate	157	50.7	151	48.4	155	47.8	7.9	12.6	2.7	(1.0)	7.9	13.1	2.6	(1.5)
Indonesia														
Total	322	100.0	356	100.0	373	100.0	10.0	28.7	4.4	17.7	16.5	27.1	4.8	15.9
Government	291	90.6	326	91.7	342	91.9	11.6	33.6	4.6	19.4	18.2	31.8	5.0	17.6
Corporate	30	9.4	29	8.3	30	8.1	(3.4)	(4.4)	2.0	1.1	2.3	(5.6)	2.3	(0.4)
Korea, Rep. of														
Total	2,424	100.0	2,365	100.0	2,388	100.0	1.2	9.4	1.5	7.9	9.0	16.3	1.0	(1.5)
Government	993	41.0	996	42.1	994	41.6	0.9	13.3	0.2	9.6	8.7	20.6	(0.2)	0.1
Corporate	1,430	59.0	1,368	57.9	1,395	58.4	1.4	6.8	2.4	6.8	9.2	13.6	1.9	(2.5)
Malaysia														
Total	399	100.0	411	100.0	417	100.0	1.3	8.0	1.0	8.2	4.7	9.9	1.5	4.4
Government	212	53.1	224	54.6	228	54.7	0.5	10.3	1.2	11.4	3.9	12.2	1.7	7.4
Corporate	187	46.9	186	45.4	189	45.3	2.2	5.6	0.8	4.6	5.7	7.4	1.3	1.0
Philippines														
Total	178	100.0	191	100.0	192	100.0	5.3	28.9	0.3	14.2	6.3	36.0	0.3	7.6
Government	145	81.2	163	85.3	164	85.5	7.0	35.3	0.5	20.3	8.0	42.7	0.6	13.3
Corporate	34	18.8	28	14.7	28	14.5	(1.3)	7.1	(1.3)	(11.8)	(0.4)	13.0	(1.2)	(17.0)
Singapore														
Total	376	100.0	430	100.0	449	100.0	3.6	10.4	3.8	21.9	7.0	12.4	4.5	19.4
Government	249	66.2	291	67.7	305	67.9	5.3	15.3	4.1	24.9	8.7	17.4	4.8	22.4
Corporate	127	33.8	139	32.3	144	32.1	0.5	1.8	3.3	16.0	3.7	3.7	4.0	13.7
Thailand														
Total	465	100.0	432	100.0	443	100.0	(0.7)	5.2	1.1	5.8	51.8	67.3	2.6	(4.6)
Government	342	73.5	313	72.5	323	72.8	(0.3)	8.3	1.6	4.7	51.1	64.2	3.1	(5.5)
Corporate	123	26.5	119	27.5	121	27.2	(1.8)	(2.5)	0.01	8.6	53.6	76.4	1.5	(2.0)
Viet Nam														
Total	72	100.0	84	100.0	92	100.0	8.1	31.4	9.8	25.5	8.5	31.8	9.5	27.0
Government	60	82.8	62	74.3	65	71.3	7.0	18.7	5.3	8.0	7.4	19.1	5.0	9.3
Corporate	12	17.2	21	25.7	26	28.7	13.9	172.4	22.7	110.0	14.3	173.3	22.3	112.5
Emerging East Asia														
Total	20,083	100.0	21,769	100.0	22,795	100.0	3.1	18.3	3.6	12.8	8.4	26.5	4.7	13.5
Government	12,423	61.9	13,580	62.4	14,291	62.7	3.6	19.6	4.0	13.9	9.0	27.9	5.2	15.0
Corporate	7,660	38.1	8,189	37.6	8,504	37.3	2.2	16.3	2.8	11.0	7.5	24.2	3.8	11.0
Japan														
Total	12,115	100.0	11,428	100.0	11,338	100.0	3.2	5.0	2.6	4.3	5.4	10.5	(0.8)	(6.4)
Government	11,250	92.9	10,601	92.8	10,515	92.7	3.3	5.1	2.6	4.2	5.5	10.5	(0.8)	(6.5)
Corporate	865	7.1	828	7.2	823	7.3	2.3	4.6	2.9	6.0	4.5	10.1	(0.5)	(4.9)
Memo Item: India														
Total	29	100.0	31	100.0	31	100.0	3.3	13.7	1.2	8.8	4.3	11.1	1.0	7.0
Government	22	77.2	24	78.0	24	78.5	3.0	15.2	1.8	10.7	4.0	12.5	1.6	8.8
Corporate	7	22.8	7	22.0	7	21.5	4.2	9.2	(1.1)	2.5	5.2	6.7	(1.2)	0.8

( ) = negative, LCY = local currency, q-o-q = quarter-on-quarter, Q3 = third quarter, Q4 = fourth quarter, USD = United States dollar, y-o-y = year-on-year.
Notes:
1. For Singapore, corporate bonds outstanding are based on *AsianBondsOnline* estimates.
2. Corporate bonds include issues by financial institutions.
3. Bloomberg LP end-of-period LCY–USD rates are used.
4. For LCY base, emerging East Asia growth figures based on 31 December 2021 currency exchange rates and do not include currency effects.
5. Emerging East Asia comprises the People's Republic of China; Hong Kong, China; Indonesia; the Republic of Korea; Malaysia; the Philippines; Singapore; Thailand; and Viet Nam.
Sources: People's Republic of China (CEIC Data Company); Hong Kong, China (Hong Kong Monetary Authority); Indonesia (Bank Indonesia; Directorate General of Budget Financing and Risk Management, Ministry of Finance; and Indonesia Stock Exchange); Republic of Korea (KG Zeroin Corporation and The Bank of Korea); Malaysia (Bank Negara Malaysia); Philippines (Bureau of the Treasury and Bloomberg LP); Singapore (Monetary Authority of Singapore, Singapore Government Securities, and Bloomberg LP); Thailand (Bank of Thailand); Viet Nam (Bloomberg LP and Vietnam Bond Market Association); Japan (Japan Securities Dealers Association); and India (Securities and Exchange Board of India and Bloomberg LP).

Figure 2: Maturity Profiles of Local Currency Government Bonds in Emerging East Asia

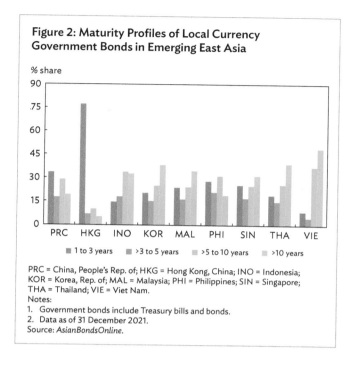

PRC = China, People's Rep. of; HKG = Hong Kong, China; INO = Indonesia; KOR = Korea, Rep. of; MAL = Malaysia; PHI = Philippines; SIN = Singapore; THA = Thailand; VIE = Viet Nam.
Notes:
1. Government bonds include Treasury bills and bonds.
2. Data as of 31 December 2021.
Source: AsianBondsOnline.

Foreign Holdings

Foreign investor ownership of government bonds increased in most emerging East Asian markets in Q4 2021.

The foreign investor holdings share increased from Q3 2021 to Q4 2021 in all emerging East Asian markets except for Indonesia, where it decreased, and for Viet Nam, where it was almost unchanged (**Figure 3**). In contrast, most markets saw quarterly declines in their foreign investor holdings share in Q3 2021. This indicates growing confidence among offshore investors as the region's economies are poised for a rebound on the back of increasing mobility levels and vaccination rates.

In the PRC, the share of foreign investor holdings increased to 10.9% at the end of December from 10.6% at the end of September. It also rose from a level of 9.7% at the end of December 2020, which was a more rapid gain compared to other markets in the region where the foreign investor holdings shares only moderately increased if not declined during the same period. The sustained increase can be explained by the fact that the share of foreign ownership is relatively low compared to most markets in the region, thus the potential for further expansion is high. Moreover, measures taken to open up the bond market and the inclusion of the PRC

Table 2: Size and Composition of Local Currency Bond Markets (% of GDP)

	Q4 2020	Q3 2021	Q4 2021
China, People's Rep. of			
Total	100.1	99.4	100.7
Government	64.3	63.8	65.0
Corporate	35.8	35.5	35.7
Hong Kong, China			
Total	89.9	86.2	88.2
Government	44.3	44.4	46.0
Corporate	45.6	41.8	42.2
Indonesia			
Total	29.3	31.0	31.3
Government	26.5	28.5	28.8
Corporate	2.8	2.6	2.5
Korea, Rep. of			
Total	143.4	148.1	148.7
Government	58.7	62.4	61.9
Corporate	84.6	85.7	86.8
Malaysia			
Total	119.4	125.2	125.3
Government	63.4	68.3	68.5
Corporate	55.9	56.8	56.8
Philippines			
Total	47.8	51.7	50.5
Government	38.8	44.1	43.1
Corporate	9.0	7.6	7.3
Singapore			
Total	104.4	112.2	113.7
Government	69.2	76.0	77.2
Corporate	35.3	36.2	36.5
Thailand			
Total	88.9	90.9	91.0
Government	65.4	65.9	66.2
Corporate	23.6	25.0	24.8
Viet Nam			
Total	26.5	23.4	24.9
Government	21.9	17.4	17.7
Corporate	4.5	6.0	7.1
Emerging East Asia			
Total	97.8	97.5	98.6
Government	60.5	60.8	61.8
Corporate	37.3	36.7	36.8
Japan			
Total	232.4	234.2	240.8
Government	215.8	217.2	223.3
Corporate	16.6	17.0	17.5

GDP = gross domestic product, Q3 = third quarter, Q4 = fourth quarter.
Notes:
1. Data for GDP is from CEIC Data Company.
2. For Singapore, corporate bonds outstanding are based on AsianBondsOnline estimates.
Sources: People's Republic of China (CEIC Data Company); Hong Kong, China (Hong Kong Monetary Authority); Indonesia (Bank Indonesia; Directorate General of Budget Financing and Risk Management, Ministry of Finance; and Indonesia Stock Exchange); Republic of Korea (KG Zeroin Corporation and The Bank of Korea); Malaysia (Bank Negara Malaysia); Philippines (Bureau of the Treasury and Bloomberg LP); Singapore (Monetary Authority of Singapore, Singapore Government Securities, and Bloomberg LP); Thailand (Bank of Thailand); Viet Nam (Bloomberg LP and Vietnam Bond Market Association); and Japan (Japan Securities Dealers Association).

Figure 3: Foreign Holdings of Local Currency Government Bonds in Select Asian Markets (% of total)

Note: Data for Japan and the Republic of Korea are as of 30 September 2021.
Source: *AsianBondsOnline* calculations based on data from local market sources.

government bonds in global bond indices, including most recently, the FTSE World Government Bond Index, are leading to more diverse opportunities for overseas investors. The attraction of the PRC's bonds was reflected in its market having the largest capital net inflows in emerging East Asia in Q4 2021.

The foreign ownership share in Malaysia's government bond market moderately increased to 26.0% at the end of December from 25.9% at the end of September. The shifting stance of the United States (US) Federal Reserve regarding future interest rate hikes may have reduced overall foreign interest in the region's LCY bonds. However, the attractive rate differential favoring Malaysian bonds eased some foreign investor aversion toward the regional market, yielding positive capital flows in Q4 2021. Lower issuance volume and a high level of maturities in the government bond market may also have contributed to the moderate increase. Malaysia has the highest foreign holdings share of LCY government bonds in the region.

The share of foreign ownership of LCY government bonds in the Philippines and Thailand increased in Q4 2021, reversing the quarterly declines in Q3 2021. In the Philippines, the share increased to 1.9% at the end of December after having fallen to 1.6% at the end of September. In Thailand, the share increased to 13.7% at the end of December after having fallen to 13.4% at the end of September. Relatively better investment conditions

amid improved growth prospects and the easing of COVID-19 restrictions prompted capital inflows to the Philippines and Thailand in Q4 2021, lifting the foreign holdings share in both markets.

In Indonesia, foreign ownership of government bonds continued to decline in Q4 2021, which was in contrast to other markets in the region. The foreign holdings share fell to 19.0% at the end of December from 21.6% at the end of September, underpinned by foreign capital outflows during Q4 2021. Even as there was less foreign investor participation, government bond issuances were being absorbed by domestic holders. In addition, the central bank continued to purchase bonds from the primary market following the extension of the burden-sharing arrangement with the government through 2022 to support the fiscal deficit. In Viet Nam, the foreign holdings share was marginally changed at 0.7% in the same review period.

The Republic of Korea saw its foreign holdings share rise to 15.9% at the end of September from 15.4% at the end of June, sustaining the upward trend in place since June 2019. Korean government bonds offer an attractive return, spurring demand overseas as evidenced by foreign investors maintaining a high net-buying position.

Foreign Fund Flows

Most emerging East Asian economies witnessed sustained foreign fund inflows into their government bond markets in Q4 2021.

Total net inflows to emerging East Asia picked up to USD36.7 billion in Q4 2021 from USD35.0 billion in Q3 2021 (**Figure 4**). Foreign investors were net buyers of the region's government bonds during the quarter. Net inflows amounted to USD6.2 billion in October, which more than doubled in November to USD14.6 billion and reached USD15.9 billion in December. The region sustained substantial foreign capital inflows into 2022, reaching USD16.2 billion in January. In February, regional net inflows totaled USD1.1 billion. Preliminary data for Indonesia and Thailand, however, showed total net outflows of USD3.0 billion in the first 9 days of March as a result of uncertainty from the Russian invasion of Ukraine.

Emerging East Asian government bonds continued to attract foreign capital as economic recovery was well underway and the COVID-19 situation was better

Figure 4: Foreign Capital Flows in Local Currency Bond Markets in Emerging East Asia

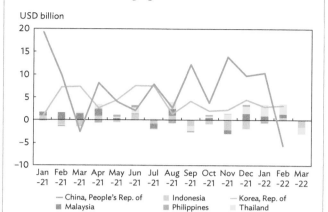

USD = United States dollar.

Notes:
1. The Republic of Korea and Thailand provided data on bond flows. For the People's Republic of China, Indonesia, Malaysia, and the Philippines, month-on-month changes in foreign holdings of local currency government bonds were used as a proxy for bond flows.
2. Data are as of 9 March 2022 except for the People's Republic of China, the Republic of Korea, and Malaysia (28 February 2022); and the Philippines (31 January 2022).
3. Figures were computed based on 9 March 2022 exchange rates to avoid currency effects.

Sources: People's Republic of China (Bloomberg LP); Indonesia (Directorate General of Budget Financing and Risk Management, Ministry of Finance); Republic of Korea (Financial Supervisory Service); Malaysia (Bank Negara Malaysia); Philippines (Bureau of the Treasury); and Thailand (Thai Bond Market Association).

managed, easing worries over monetary normalization by major central banks. While yields have been rising in developed markets, interest rate differentials that favor emerging East Asia continued to play a major factor in foreign investor decisions to direct funds into the region's bond market. Moreover, the Federal Reserve's tapering and normalization process is being carried out in a transparent and properly communicated manner, preventing a sudden reversal of capital flows.

Foreign fund inflows in the PRC amounted to USD27.5 billion in Q4 2021, up from USD22.9 billion in the previous quarter. The largest monthly net inflows were posted in November, amounting to USD13.9 billion, nearly quadruple the amount in October. November was the first month of PRC government bonds' inclusion in the FTSE Russell's World Government Index. In January, the PRC government bond market drew in USD10.4 billion of foreign funds. Favorable returns due to slowing domestic inflation and a stable Chinese yuan were catalysts for the sustained foreign interest in the government bond market. However, the PRC had a reversal in February, recording net outflows of USD5.6 billion.

In the Republic of Korea, net inflows slowed to USD8.8 billion in Q4 2021 from USD13.1 billion in Q3 2021. Foreign buying of Korean government bonds diminished quarterly throughout 2021 after rebounding in the first quarter of the year. Net inflows in October amounted to USD2.0 billion and turned more than double in December to USD4.5 billion. The Republic of Korea attracted USD3.0 billion and USD3.2 billion worth of foreign funds in January and February, respectively. Surging inflation and the Bank of Korea's interest rate hikes may have capped foreign investors' appetite for the securities. Nonetheless, the Korean bond market remained the second-largest destination of foreign funds in the region.

Improved growth prospects brought by increased economic activities and the easing of COVID-19 curbs drove larger net foreign fund inflows to the markets of Malaysia, the Philippines, and Thailand. In Malaysia, foreign funds invested in government bonds increased to USD1.2 billion in Q4 2021 from USD0.7 billion in Q3 2021. Net outflows from the Philippines of USD1.2 billion in Q3 2021 reversed to inflows of USD0.7 billion in Q4 2021. In Thailand, net inflows jumped from USD0.6 billion to USD3.4 billion during the same period. The Federal Reserve's announcement that it would start tapering its bond purchases in November may have adversely affected foreign investor sentiment toward the Malaysian and Philippine markets, as Malaysia posted a sell-off during the month while the Philippines saw a decline in net inflows; both markets recovered in December. Thailand continued to attract strong interest, recording net inflows of USD2.4 billion and USD2.2 billion in January and February, respectively. Malaysia also posted net inflows albeit at lower levels of USD1.0 billion and USD0.7 billion in the same period. In the Philippines, rising COVID-19 cases may have led to net outflows of USD0.3 billion in January.

Indonesia was the only market in emerging East Asia that experienced net foreign fund outflows in Q4 2021. It posted net outflows of USD4.9 billion, larger than the net outflows of USD1.1 billion in the previous quarter. In all 3 months of Q4 2021, Indonesia recorded net outflows. In January 2022, foreign investors sold a net USD0.3 billion. However, this reconciles with the government's move to develop the domestic investor base and rely less on foreign funds. Indonesia, however, recorded net fund inflows of USD0.7 billion for the month of February. High levels of liquidity generated by domestic investors provide support to the development of the Indonesian government bond market.

LCY Bond Issuance

The issuance volume of LCY bonds in emerging East Asia totaled USD9.0 trillion in 2021.

Issuance of LCY bonds in emerging East Asia continued its upward trajectory in 2021, with regional markets focused on strengthening economic recovery amid the COVID-19 outbreak. Issuance in 2021 surpassed that of 2020, marking the highest annual issuance to date for the region. Aggregate issuance of LCY bonds in emerging East Asia reached USD9.0 trillion for full-year 2021, up by 7.1% y-o-y from USD8.4 billion in 2020 (**Figure 5**). ASEAN member economies accounted for a 17.0% share of the regional issuance total in 2021, with their share rising from 14.7% in 2020. The PRC; Hong Kong, China; and the Republic of Korea saw declines in their corresponding shares to 67.7%, 6.3%, and 9.0%, respectively.

Strong momentum in issuance was buoyed by increased issuance in all bond segments. Government bonds and corporate bonds accounted for most of the issuance volume, representing shares of 40.7% and 42.0%, respectively, of the 2021 issuance total (**Figure 6**). Central bank issuance accounted for the remaining 17.2% share. Strong government bond issuance continued due to the need to support pandemic response measures,

while improving economic optimism led to increased corporate bond issuance.

Quarterly issuance volumes were broadly steady in 2021. In Q4 2021, total LCY bond issuance in the region tallied USD2.4 trillion, inching up from USD2.3 trillion in Q3 2021 (**Table 3**). Issuance growth was positive in six out of nine emerging East Asian markets in Q4 2021 compared with Q3 2021, including Hong Kong, China; Indonesia; the Republic of Korea; Malaysia; Singapore; and Viet Nam. On the other hand, q-o-q contractions in issuance volume were noted in the PRC, the Philippines, and Thailand.

Overall issuance growth in the region's LCY bond market moderated to 0.2% q-o-q in Q4 2021 from 5.1% q-o-q in Q3 2021, dragged down by a 9.6% q-o-q contraction in the issuance of Treasury and other government bonds. Most governments had already fulfilled their borrowing needs, leading to reduced issuance volume during the quarter. In addition, issuance was somewhat curtailed as investors sought higher yields, driven by shifting US monetary policy. Nonetheless, issuance of Treasury and other government bonds was still substantial in Q4 2021 at USD912.2 billion. The only regional markets that had increased issuance of Treasury and other government bonds in Q4 2021 versus Q3 2021 were Indonesia, Singapore, and Thailand. Treasury and other government bonds accounted for 38.5% of the region's aggregate issuance in Q4 2021.

Figure 5: Local Currency Bond Issuance in Emerging East Asia

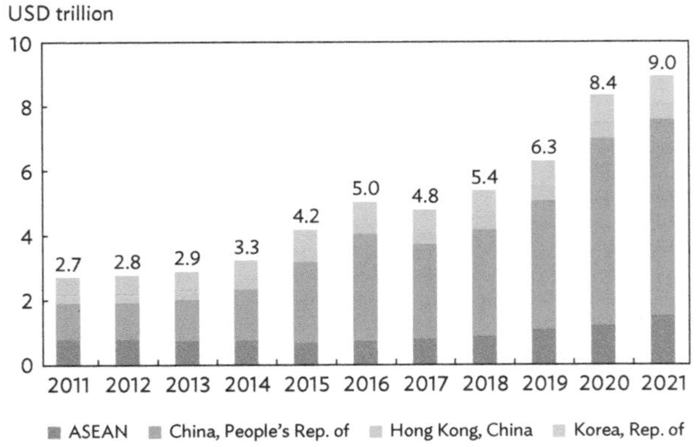

USD trillion

[Bar chart showing LCY bond issuance from 2011 to 2021: 2011 = 2.7, 2012 = 2.8, 2013 = 2.9, 2014 = 3.3, 2015 = 4.2, 2016 = 5.0, 2017 = 4.8, 2018 = 5.4, 2019 = 6.3, 2020 = 8.4, 2021 = 9.0]

■ ASEAN ■ China, People's Rep. of ■ Hong Kong, China ■ Korea, Rep. of

ASEAN = Association of Southeast Asian Nations, USD = United States dollar.
Notes:
1. ASEAN includes the markets of Indonesia, Malaysia, the Philippines, Singapore, Thailand, and Viet Nam.
2. Figures were computed based on 31 December 2021 currency exchange rates and do not include currency effects.
Source: *AsianBondsOnline*.

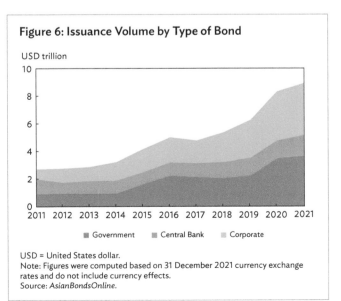

Figure 6: Issuance Volume by Type of Bond

USD trillion

■ Government ■ Central Bank ■ Corporate

USD = United States dollar.
Note: Figures were computed based on 31 December 2021 currency exchange rates and do not include currency effects.
Source: *AsianBondsOnline*.

Table 3: Local-Currency–Denominated Bond Issuance (gross)

	Q4 2020		Q3 2021		Q4 2021		Growth Rate (LCY-base %)		Growth Rate (USD-base %)	
							Q4 2021		Q4 2021	
	Amount (USD billion)	% share	Amount (USD billion)	% share	Amount (USD billion)	% share	q-o-q	y-o-y	q-o-q	y-o-y
China, People's Rep. of										
Total	1,294	100.0	1,629	100.0	1,598	100.0	(3.2)	20.3	(1.9)	23.5
Government	590	45.6	848	52.1	775	48.5	(9.8)	27.9	(8.6)	31.3
Central Bank	0	0.0	0	0.0	0	0.0	–	–	–	–
Treasury and Other Govt.	590	45.6	848	52.1	775	48.5	(9.8)	27.9	(8.6)	31.3
Corporate	703	54.4	781	47.9	823	51.5	3.9	13.9	5.3	17.0
Hong Kong, China										
Total	146	100.0	139	100.0	144	100.0	4.0	(1.1)	3.9	(1.6)
Government	112	76.3	113	81.8	118	81.7	4.0	6.0	3.8	5.4
Central Bank	107	73.1	109	78.9	117	81.1	6.9	9.7	6.7	9.1
Treasury and Other Govt.	5	3.2	4	2.9	1	0.7	(75.8)	(79.5)	(75.8)	(79.6)
Corporate	35	23.7	25	18.2	26	18.3	4.2	(23.8)	4.0	(24.2)
Indonesia										
Total	47	100.0	48	100.0	49	100.0	1.4	4.9	1.7	3.3
Government	46	96.8	46	95.2	47	95.5	1.7	3.5	2.0	2.0
Central Bank	14	29.7	27	57.0	28	57.4	2.0	102.7	2.4	99.7
Treasury and Other Govt.	32	67.1	18	38.2	19	38.1	1.1	(40.4)	1.4	(41.3)
Corporate	2	3.2	2	4.8	2	4.5	(4.4)	45.1	(4.0)	42.9
Korea, Rep. of										
Total	210	100.0	180	100.0	205	100.0	14.3	6.6	13.7	(2.6)
Government	78	37.2	78	43.4	60	29.4	(22.5)	(15.6)	(22.9)	(22.9)
Central Bank	29	13.8	27	15.0	21	10.3	(21.2)	(20.2)	(21.6)	(27.2)
Treasury and Other Govt.	49	23.4	51	28.4	39	19.1	(23.2)	(12.9)	(23.5)	(20.5)
Corporate	132	62.8	102	56.6	144	70.6	42.5	19.8	41.8	9.4
Malaysia										
Total	22	100.0	21	100.0	21	100.0	2.6	(0.7)	1.6	(4.7)
Government	8	35.1	12	55.9	11	53.7	(1.3)	51.9	(2.3)	45.9
Central Bank	0	0.0	0	0.0	0	0.0	–	–	–	–
Treasury and Other Govt.	8	35.1	12	55.9	11	53.7	(1.3)	51.9	(2.3)	45.9
Corporate	14	64.9	9	44.1	10	46.3	7.6	(29.2)	6.5	(32.0)
Philippines										
Total	29	100.0	42	100.0	39	100.0	(7.0)	43.2	(7.0)	34.9
Government	28	95.8	41	97.7	38	97.1	(7.6)	45.2	(7.6)	36.7
Central Bank	17	60.2	26	62.3	24	60.0	(10.4)	42.9	(10.4)	34.6
Treasury and Other Govt.	10	35.6	15	35.4	15	37.0	(2.6)	49.1	(2.6)	40.4
Corporate	1	4.2	1	2.3	1	2.9	18.4	(0.9)	18.4	(6.7)
Singapore										
Total	164	100.0	205	100.0	244	100.0	18.0	52.0	18.7	48.9
Government	160	97.9	200	97.4	240	98.2	19.0	52.4	19.7	49.3
Central Bank	135	82.5	174	84.8	211	86.3	20.1	59.1	20.9	55.9
Treasury and Other Govt.	25	15.5	26	12.6	29	11.9	11.4	16.7	12.1	14.4
Corporate	3	2.1	5	2.6	4	1.8	(18.6)	31.9	(18.1)	29.3
Thailand										
Total	74	100.0	69	100.0	62	100.0	(12.5)	(8.3)	(11.2)	(17.3)
Government	65	87.6	55	79.9	50	82.1	(10.1)	(14.1)	(8.8)	(22.5)
Central Bank	49	66.4	37	53.4	31	50.9	(16.6)	(29.8)	(15.4)	(36.7)
Treasury and Other Govt.	16	21.2	18	26.5	19	31.2	3.0	35.0	4.5	21.8
Corporate	9	12.4	14	20.1	11	17.9	(22.1)	32.4	(20.9)	19.4

continued on next page

Table 3 *continued*

| | Q4 2020 | | Q3 2021 | | Q4 2021 | | Growth Rate (LCY-base %) | | Growth Rate (USD-base %) | |
| | | | | | | | Q4 2021 | | Q4 2021 | |
	Amount (USD billion)	% share	Amount (USD billion)	% share	Amount (USD billion)	% share	q-o-q	y-o-y	q-o-q	y-o-y
Viet Nam										
Total	7	100.0	9	100.0	9	100.0	5.8	25.4	5.5	26.9
Government	5	73.3	5	52.9	4	42.4	(15.1)	(27.4)	(15.4)	(26.6)
Central Bank	0	0.0	0	0.0	0	0.0	–	–	–	–
Treasury and Other Govt.	5	73.3	5	52.9	4	42.4	(15.1)	(27.4)	(15.4)	(26.6)
Corporate	2	26.7	4	47.1	5	57.6	29.4	170.8	29.1	174.1
Emerging East Asia										
Total	1,994	100.0	2,342	100.0	2,371	100.0	0.2	18.8	1.2	18.9
Government	1,093	54.8	1,398	59.7	1,344	56.7	(4.8)	23.4	(3.9)	22.9
Central Bank	352	17.7	401	17.1	431	18.2	7.1	26.8	7.5	22.5
Treasury and Other Govt.	741	37.1	997	42.6	912	38.5	(9.6)	21.8	(8.5)	23.2
Corporate	902	45.2	944	40.3	1,027	43.3	7.6	13.2	8.8	13.9
Japan										
Total	771	100.0	502	100.0	662	100.0	36.2	(4.3)	31.7	(14.2)
Government	718	93.2	464	92.5	615	93.0	36.9	(4.6)	32.4	(14.4)
Central Bank	0	0.0	10	2.0	0	0.0	(100.0)	–	–	–
Treasury and Other Govt.	718	93.2	454	90.5	615	93.0	40.0	(4.6)	35.4	(14.4)
Corporate	53	6.8	38	7.5	47	7.0	27.7	(1.2)	23.5	(11.4)

( ) = negative, – = not applicable, LCY = local currency, q-o-q = quarter-on-quarter, Q3 = third quarter, Q4 = fourth quarter, USD = United States dollar, y-o-y = year-on-year.
Notes:
1. Corporate bonds include issues by financial institutions.
2. Bloomberg LP end-of-period LCY–USD rates are used.
3. For LCY base, emerging East Asia growth figures are based on 31 December 2021 currency exchange rates and do not include currency effects.
Sources: People's Republic of China (CEIC Data Company); Hong Kong, China (Hong Kong Monetary Authority); Indonesia (Bank Indonesia; Directorate General of Budget Financing and Risk Management, Ministry of Finance; and Indonesia Stock Exchange); Republic of Korea (KG Zeroin Corporation and The Bank of Korea); Malaysia (Bank Negara Malaysia); Philippines (Bureau of the Treasury and Bloomberg LP); Singapore (Singapore Government Securities and Bloomberg LP); Thailand (Bank of Thailand); Viet Nam (Bloomberg LP, Hanoi Stock Exchange, and Vietnam Bond Market Association); and Japan (Japan Securities Dealers Association).

In Q4 2021, growth in the issuance of central bank instruments eased to 7.1% q-o-q in Q4 2021 from 8.6% q-o-q in the preceding quarter. Total central bank issuance during the quarter stood at USD431.3 billion, accounting for an 18.2% share of emerging East Asia's total issuance.

Corporate bonds continued to account for the largest share of issuance during the quarter with volume reaching USD1,027.4 billion, representing a 43.3% share of the regional issuance total. Growth in corporate bond issuance quickened to 7.6% q-o-q from 5.1% q-o-q in Q3 2021. Issuance during the quarter was active in most markets, with corporates taking advantage of still low borrowing cost in anticipation of rising interest rates. Six markets in the region recorded higher volume of issuance in Q4 2021: the PRC; Hong Kong, China; the Republic of Korea; Malaysia; the Philippines; and Viet Nam.

The y-o-y issuance growth in emerging East Asia swelled to 18.8% in Q4 2021 from only 0.8% in Q3 2021. The bond markets of the PRC, Indonesia, the Republic of Korea, the

Philippines, Singapore, and Viet Nam recorded positive y-o-y expansions in Q4 2021, while contractions were observed in Hong Kong, China; Malaysia; and Thailand. Treasury and other government bond issuance rebounded with a 21.8% y-o-y hike following a decline of 7.6% y-o-y in Q3 2021. Central bank issuance growth accelerated to 26.8% y-o-y in Q4 2021 from 19.0% y-o-y in Q3 2021, while corporate bond issuance growth climbed to 13.2% y-o-y from 4.1% y-o-y over the same period.

The PRC's bond issuance declined 3.2% q-o-q in Q4 2021 to USD1.6 trillion as government bond issuance fell 9.8% q-o-q. While Treasury bond issuance gained 11.2% q-o-q, government bond issuance was dragged down by the 16.5% q-o-q decline in local government bond issuance and a 28.0% q-o-q decline in policy bank bond issuance. The slowdown in local government bond issuance was due to high issuance in July–October as local governments sought to complete their issuance quotas. Issuance volume markedly dropped in November and December. In contrast, corporate bond issuance growth slowed to 3.9% q-o-q from 11.5% q-o-q due to economic growth concerns and negative sentiments over property default issues. On a y-o-y basis, overall issuance rose 20.3% in Q4 2021 after contracting 1.7% in Q3 2021.

In the Republic of Korea, total issuance during the quarter rose to USD204.6 billion, on growth of 14.3% q-o-q. Overall issuance was pulled down by a deceleration in the issuance of government bonds, which contracted 22.5% q-o-q. Issuance of instruments from the Bank of Korea, as well as Treasury and other government bonds, fell in Q4 2021 for the second quarter in a row, following a high volume of borrowing in the first half of the year. In contrast, issuance of corporate bonds was robust during the quarter, as firms engaged in borrowings ahead of market expectations that the Bank of Korea would further raise policy rates. (The Bank of Korea previously raised policy rates in August 2021, November 2021, and January 2022.) On an annual basis, LCY bond sales in the Republic of Korea grew 6.6% y-o-y in Q4 2021 after a 3.7% y-o-y contraction in Q3 2021.

LCY bond issuance in Hong Kong, China rebounded strongly in Q4 2021 to USD144.0 billion, posting growth of 4.0% q-o-q after a 0.8% q-o-q decline in Q3 2021. Growth was largely driven by increased issuance of central bank instruments, particularly EFBs. The Hong Kong Monetary Authority raised its planned issuance of EFBs in each month from September through December due to abundant liquidity in the banking system. This led central bank issuance growth during the quarter to rise to 6.9% q-o-q from 3.0% q-o-q in Q3 2021. In contrast, issuance of Hong Kong Special Administrative Region bonds substantially dropped by 75.8% q-o-q. Corporate bond issuance rebounded, rising 4.2% q-o-q following a decline of 15.8% q-o-q in Q3 2021. On a y-o-y basis, Hong Kong, China's bond issuance declined at a slower pace of 1.1% in Q4 2021 versus a 3.7% drop in Q3 2021.

The aggregate LCY bond sales of ASEAN members reached USD424.1 billion in Q4 2021. ASEAN bond issuance accounted for a 17.9% share of emerging East Asia's total issuance volume during the quarter, up from 16.8% in Q3 2021. Issuance growth inched up to 6.8% q-o-q in Q4 2021 from 6.3% q-o-q in Q3 2021. On an annual basis, issuance growth expanded by a much faster 28.3% y-o-y in Q4 2021 than the 18.1% y-o-y registered in the previous quarter. The markets of Indonesia, Malaysia, Singapore, and Viet Nam engaged in more borrowing in Q4 2021 than in Q3 2021, while the Philippines and Thailand engaged in less bond issuance. Among all ASEAN members, the three largest issuers of

LCY bonds during the quarter were Singapore, Thailand, and Indonesia, accounting for 57.5%, 14.5%, and 11.5%, respectively, of ASEAN's issuance total in Q4 2021.

Singapore's Q4 2021 LCY bond issuance reached USD243.9 billion, gaining 18.0% q-o-q versus 6.7% q-o-q in Q3 2021. Singapore's LCY bond issuance growth came solely from the government bond sector, with issuance rising 19.0% q-o-q, while corporate bond issuance fell 18.6% q-o-q. Central bank bond issuance was the biggest driver in Singapore's government bond sector, gaining 20.1% q-o-q as the central bank sought to limit inflationary pressure. LCY bond issuance in Singapore climbed the fastest among regional markets, with growth of 52.0% y-o-y in Q4 2021.

Thailand's LCY bond issuance fell 12.5% q-o-q to USD61.5 billion in Q4 2021, driven by quarterly declines in both the government and corporate bond sectors. Government bond issuance fell 10.1% q-o-q due to a 16.6.% q-o-q decline in central bank issuance, as the Bank of Thailand pledged more support for COVID-19 relief measures. Treasury bonds and other government bond issuance rose 3.0% q-o-q in Q4 2021, while corporate bond issuance fell 22.1% q-o-q. On an annual basis, Thailand's LCY bond issuance declined 8.3% y-o-y in Q4 2021 due to the decline in central bank issuance.

In Indonesia, issuance growth moderated to 1.4% q-o-q in Q4 2021 from 22.5% q-o-q in Q3 2021. Total issuance volume reached USD48.7 billion during the quarter, with government bonds accounting for a 95.5% share. Overall growth in government bonds decelerated to 1.7% q-o-q in Q4 2021 from 20.7% q-o-q in Q3 2021. Bank Indonesia continued to actively issue Sukuk Bank Indonesia, yet growth moderated to 2.0% q-o-q in Q4 2021. Issuance of Treasury bills and bonds in Q4 2021 also eased to 1.1% q-o-q from 13.3% q-o-q in the earlier quarter, as the government cancelled all remaining scheduled auctions after 2 November due to adequate funding for its budgetary needs. Corporate bond issuance declined 4.4% q-o-q in Q4 2021 following a 73.3% q-o-q hike in the preceding quarter. On an annual basis, issuance growth eased to 4.9% y-o-y in Q4 2021 from 11.3% y-o-y in Q3 2021.

LCY bond sales in the Philippines declined to USD39.2 billion in Q4 2021, falling 7.0% q-o-q after posting growth of 4.5% q-o-q in the preceding quarter. Overall, growth was dragged down by a slowdown in the issuance of government bonds, which declined 7.6% q-o-q in Q4 2021. Both the issuance of Bangko Sentral ng Pilipinas bills (–10.4% q-o-q) and Treasury and other government bonds (–2.6% q-o-q) contracted during the quarter. The Bureau of the Treasury scaled back its issuance of Treasury bills and bonds in December and also allowed more outstanding bonds to mature. This was undertaken to allow the debt-to-GDP ratio to fall below 60% at the end of 2021. The corporate bond segment was the sole driver of growth in the Philippines, as issuance growth surged to 18.4% q-o-q in Q4 2021 from 5.1% q-o-q in Q3 2021. On a y-o-y basis, the growth in LCY bond issuance moderated to 43.2% in Q4 2021 from 74.4% in the prior quarter.

LCY bond issuance in Malaysia tallied USD21.3 billion in Q4 2021 on growth of 2.6% q-o-q. Similar to the Philippines, corporate bonds drove issuance growth during the quarter as government issuance fell 1.3% q-o-q in Q4 2021 on the back of a 13.4% q-o-q decline in Q3 2021. Issuance volume was dampened as investors sought higher rates after the US Federal Reserve's tapering announcement. Corporate bond issuance grew 7.6% q-o-q following a decline of 15.3% q-o-q in Q3 2021. On a y-o-y basis, LCY bond issuance growth in Malaysia declined at a slower pace of 0.7% versus a 3.5% drop in Q3 2021.

Viet Nam's LCY bond issuance totaled USD9.4 billion Q4 2021 on a 5.8% q-o-q gain. Growth in Viet Nam's bond issuance was solely due to a 29.4% q-o-q increase in corporate issuance to USD5.4 billion on optimism over Viet Nam's economy. Viet Nam's GDP grew 5.2% y-o-y in Q4 2021, bouncing back from Q3 2021's 6.2% y-o-y decline. In contrast, government bond issuance fell 15.1% q-o-q after Viet Nam failed to meet its auction targets as market participants sought higher yields. On a y-o-y basis, Viet Nam's bond issuance grew 25.4% in Q4 2021.

Cross-Border Bond Issuance

Emerging East Asia's cross-border bond issuance fell to USD4.4 billion in Q4 2021.

Emerging East Asia's cross-border bond issuance totaled USD4.4 billion in Q4 2021, a 35.9% q-o-q decline from the USD6.9 billion raised in the previous quarter. The lower issuance volume for the quarter can be attributed to rising yields in the region, which made it costly for firms to raise funds via bond issuance, and with firms having already met their borrowing requirements for the year. Institutions from four regional economies issued cross-border bonds in Q4 2021, with a large majority continuing to come from Hong Kong, China. Other

economies that registered issuance of cross-border bonds were Singapore, Malaysia, and the Republic of Korea. Monthly issuance volumes amounted to USD1.8 billion, USD1.7 billion, and USD0.9 billion for the months of October, November, and December, respectively. Compared with the same period in 2020, total intra-regional bond issuance increased almost four-fold in Q4 2021 from USD1.2 billion.

Hong Kong, China remained home to the largest cross-border issuance volume in the region with a market share of 83.7% in Q4 2021, a reflection of its developed bond market infrastructure that makes it more accessible and efficient for firms to issue cross-border bonds (**Figure 7**). Aggregate issuance for the quarter reached USD3.7 billion; however, this was a 31.5% q-o-q decline from USD5.4 billion in Q3 2021. Sixteen firms issued cross-border bonds in Q4 2021, which were all denominated in Chinese yuan except for one which was in Singapore dollars. Financial companies and Hong Kong, China's government led the issuance of cross-border bonds in Q4 2021, with shares of 29.6% and 21.1%, respectively. The government was the single-largest issuer in both Hong Kong, China and in the entire region in Q4 2021, with a total issuance volume of USD775.8 million. The issuances were denominated in Chinese yuan in two tranches with tenors of 3 years (CNY2.5 billion) and 5 years (CNY2.5 billion). The bond offer was also the government's inaugural offering of offshore yuan bonds and was part of the government's Green Bond Programme. Shenzhen International Holdings, which invests in and operates logistics and toll road infrastructure, raised USD620.7 million via

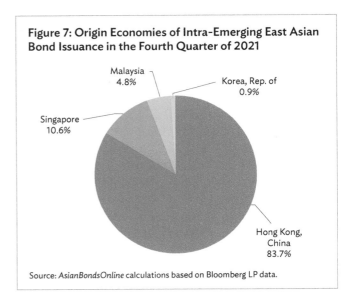

Figure 7: Origin Economies of Intra-Emerging East Asian Bond Issuance in the Fourth Quarter of 2021

Malaysia 4.8%
Korea, Rep. of 0.9%
Singapore 10.6%
Hong Kong, China 83.7%

Source: *AsianBondsOnline* calculations based on Bloomberg LP data.

issuance of 6-year CNY-denominated bonds. It was also the second-largest aggregate issuer of cross-border bonds and had the single-largest issuance in both Hong Kong, China and the region in Q4 2021. Another notable issuer was China Power International, which also had the second-largest aggregate issuance, raised USD620.7 million via issuance of 6-month and 3-year CNY-denominated bonds.

In Singapore, four firms issued cross-border bonds in Q4 2021 with a total volume of USD463.8 million, which was more than double the USD219.9 million raised in the previous quarter. Asia Water Technology led all issuers with USD232.7 million worth of 5-year CNY-denominated bonds. A financial company, Ascendas REIT, raised USD122.0 million via 10-year HKD-denominated bonds. Trafigura Group, involved in commodities trading, issued USD108.6 million worth of 3-year Chinese yuan bonds. Meanwhile, Nomura International Fund raised a total of USD0.4 million via issuance of 5-year CNY-denominated bonds.

In Malaysia, only two institutions issued intra-regional bonds in Q4 2021 with an aggregate amount of USD212.5 million. Cagamas Global, a state-owned mortgage corporation, raised USD147.3 million via issuance of 2-year bonds denominated in Singapore dollars. Malayan Banking issued a total of USD65.2 million worth of 3-year CNY-denominated bonds.

The Export–Import Bank of Korea was the sole issuer of intra-regional bonds from the Republic of Korea in

Q4 2021, raising USD39.2 million worth of 2-year bonds denominated in Philippine pesos.

The top 10 issuers of intra-regional bonds in Q4 2021 reached an aggregate volume of USD3.6 billion and comprised 81.4% of the regional total. Eight of the firms were from Hong Kong, China and had total issuance of USD3.2 billion, led by the Government of the Hong Kong Special Administrative Region of the PRC; Shenzhen International Holdings; and China Power International. Other firms in the list were from Singapore (Asia Water Technology) and Malaysia (Cagamas Global).

The Chinese yuan continued to be the most widely used currency for cross-border bonds in Q4 2021 with an aggregate issuance volume of USD4.0 billion, accounting for a share of 91.2% of the regional total (**Figure 8**). Firms from Hong Kong, China; Malaysia; and Singapore issued in Chinese yuan. Other currencies used were the Singapore dollar (5.1%, USD224.6 million), Hong Kong dollar (2.8%, USD122.0 million), and Philippine peso (0.9%, USD39.2 million).

In Q4 2021, financial companies remained the largest issuer group of cross-border bonds in emerging East Asia, with an aggregate volume of USD1.5 billion, comprising a third of the regional total (**Figure 9**). The Bank of China Group was the largest issuer from the finance sector with total volume of USD310.3 million, followed by the

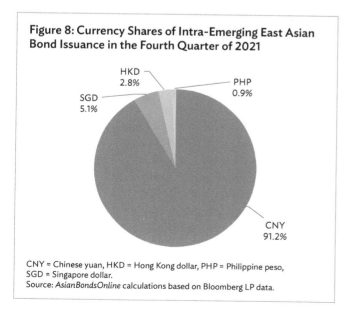

Figure 8: Currency Shares of Intra-Emerging East Asian Bond Issuance in the Fourth Quarter of 2021

CNY = Chinese yuan, HKD = Hong Kong dollar, PHP = Philippine peso, SGD = Singapore dollar.
Source: *AsianBondsOnline* calculations based on Bloomberg LP data.

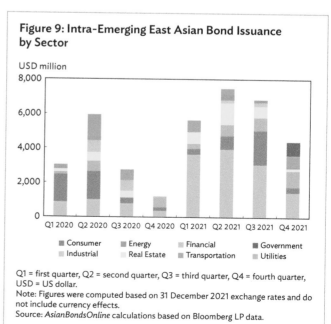

Figure 9: Intra-Emerging East Asian Bond Issuance by Sector

Q1 = first quarter, Q2 = second quarter, Q3 = third quarter, Q4 = fourth quarter, USD = US dollar.
Note: Figures were computed based on 31 December 2021 exchange rates and do not include currency effects.
Source: *AsianBondsOnline* calculations based on Bloomberg LP data.

Hong Kong Mortgage Corporation with USD257.6 million. Utility companies were the second-largest issuer group in Q4 2021 with total issuance of USD969.8 million and a regional share of 22.1%. It was the only group that posted a quarterly increase in its regional issuance share from Q3 2021. The notable issuers from this group were China Power International Development and Asia Water Technology. The third-largest group was the government sector at USD775.8 million and a 17.7% share, with the government in Hong Kong, China as the sole issuer. The transportation sector also had a notable share of 14.1% and an issuance volume of USD620.7 million, with Shenzhen International Holdings as the sole issuer of cross-border bonds from this sector in Q4 2021.

G3 Currency Bond Issuance

Emerging East Asia's G3 currency bond issuance totaled USD376.4 billion in 2021.

Issuance of G3 currency bonds in emerging East Asia totaled USD376.4 billion in 2021, a contraction of 0.5% y-o-y from USD378.1 billion in 2020 (**Table 4**).[4] The slightly smaller issuance amount was the result of most of the region's economies having less G3 bond issuance in 2021 compared to the previous year due to rising US dollar interest rates.

In 2021, 91.4% of the total issuance of G3 currency bonds was in US dollars, 8.0% in euros, and 0.6% in Japanese yen. The value of USD-denominated bonds issued in emerging East Asia in 2021 was USD344.0 billion, a 1.0% y-o-y decrease from the previous year. Most economies in the region had less US dollar issuance in 2021 than in 2020, led by the PRC whose issuance declined by USD12.6 billion. Funds raised in euros totaled USD30.2 billion in 2021, growing 7.2% y-o-y due to increased issuance activities in Hong Kong, China; Indonesia; the Republic of Korea; the Philippines; and Singapore. Proceeds from bonds issued in Japanese yen amounted to USD2.2 billion, falling 7.8% y-o-y because of large declines in Hong Kong, China's and Malaysia's issuance during the year.

More than 50.0% of the G3 currency bonds issued in the region came from entities in the PRC, which issued a total of USD217.4 billion worth in 2021. This was followed

by the Republic of Korea with USD43.9 billion and Hong Kong, China with USD39.7 billion. All economies in the region used the US dollar as their main G3 currency of choice in 2021.

In 2021, y-o-y declines in the issuance of G3 currency bonds were recorded in the Philippines (–30.0%), Thailand (–23.0%), Malaysia (–7.1%), the PRC (–6.4%), and Indonesia (–5.2%). The drop in the PRC's issuance was due to government efforts to rein in credit risk and uncertainties over bond defaults. Annual growth in G3 currency bond issuance was posted in Viet Nam (1,868.8%); the Republic of Korea (46.3%); Singapore (11.8%); and Hong Kong, China (14.0%). Cambodia did not issue any G3 currency bonds in 2021 after issuing USD350.0 million in 2020.

In 2021, 57.8% of all G3 currency bond issuance in emerging East Asia was from the PRC. Of this, USD203.2 billion was issued in US dollars and the equivalent of USD14.2 billion was issued in euros. In October, the Government of the PRC issued a four-tranche USD-denominated bond worth USD4.0 billion and with maturities of 3 years, 5 years, 10 years, and 30 years. Proceeds from the issuance will be used for general government purposes. The following month it issued three tranches of bonds denominated in euros totaling USD4.5 billion and with tenors of 3 years, 7 years, and 12 years. The issuances aimed to improve benchmark rates for offshore bonds issued by the PRC. Also in November, NXP Semiconductors NV, through its subsidiaries, raised USD2.0 billion from a triple-tranche USD-denominated bond issuance with tenors of 10 years, 20 years, and 30 years. The funds raised will be used to redeem some of the company's existing debts and for general corporate purposes.

During the review period, the Republic of Korea accounted for 11.7% of all issuance of G3 currency bonds in the region: USD37.8 billion was issued in US dollars, the equivalent of USD6.0 billion in EUR-denominated bonds, and USD0.1 billion in Japanese yen. In October, Kookmin Bank issued USD568.5 million worth of 5-year EUR-denominated bonds with a coupon rate of 0.048%. The commercial bank also issued seven USD-denominated bonds in Q4 2021 with tenors of 1 year and 2 years. Korea Housing Finance Corporate issued a USD625.4 million EUR-denominated sustainable

---

4 G3 currency bonds are denominated in either euros, Japanese yen, or US dollars. For the discussion on G3 currency issuance, emerging East Asia comprises Cambodia; the People's Republic of China; Hong Kong, China; Indonesia; the Republic of Korea; Malaysia; the Philippines; Singapore; Thailand; and Viet Nam.

Table 4: G3 Currency Bond Issuance

2020			2021		
Issuer	Amount (USD billion)	Issue Date	Issuer	Amount (USD billion)	Issue Date
Cambodia	0.4		Cambodia	0.0	
China, People's Rep. of	232.3		China, People's Rep. of	217.4	
Industrial and Commercial Bank of China 3.58% Perpetual	2.9	23-Sep-20	Industrial and Commercial Bank of China 3.200% Perpetual	6.2	24-Sep-21
Bank of China 3.60% Perpetual	2.8	4-Mar-20	China Development Bank 0.380% 2022	2.0	10-Jun-21
Bank of Communications 3.80% Perpetual	2.8	18-Nov-20	Prosus 3.061% 2031	1.9	13-Jul-21
Others	223.8		Others	207.4	
Hong Kong, China	34.8		Hong Kong, China	39.7	
AIA Group 3.200% 2040	1.8	16-Sep-20	Hong Kong, China (Sovereign) 0.000% 2026	1.4	24-Nov-21
MTR Corporation 1.625% 2030	1.2	19-Aug-20	NWD Finance 4.125% Perpetual	1.2	10-Jun-21
AIA Group 3.375% 2030	1.0	7-Apr-20	Hong Kong, China (Sovereign) 0.625% 2026	1.0	2-Feb-21
Others	30.9		Others	36.1	
Indonesia	27.9		Indonesia	26.4	
Indonesia (Sovereign) 3.85% 2030	1.7	15-Apr-20	Indonesia (Sovereign) 3.05% 2051	2.0	12-Jan-21
Indonesia (Sovereign) 4.20% 2050	1.7	15-Apr-20	Perusahaan Penerbit SBSN Indonesia III 1.50% 2026	1.3	9-Jun-21
Indonesia (Sovereign) 0.90% 2027	1.2	14-Jan-20	Indonesia (Sovereign) 1.85% 2031	1.3	12-Jan-21
Others	23.4		Others	21.9	
Korea, Rep. of	30.0		Korea, Rep. of	43.9	
Korea Housing Finance Corporation 0.010% 2025	1.2	5-Feb-20	Posco 0.00% 2026	1.2	1-Sep-21
Korea Development Bank 1.250% 2025	1.0	3-Jun-20	Korea Housing Finance Corporation 0.01% 2026	1.1	29-Jun-21
Export–Import Bank of Korea 0.829% 2025	0.9	27-Apr-20	SK Hynix 1.50% 2026	1.0	19-Jan-21
Others	26.9		Others	40.6	
Malaysia	17.2		Malaysia	16.0	
Petronas Capital 4.55% 2050	2.8	21-Apr-20	Petronas Capital 3.404% 2061	1.8	28-Apr-21
Petronas Capital 3.50% 2030	2.3	21-Apr-20	Petronas Capital 2.480% 2032	1.3	28-Apr-21
Others	12.2		Others	13.0	
Philippines	15.5		Philippines	10.8	
Philippines (Sovereign) 2.65% 2045	1.5	10-Dec-20	Philippines (Sovereign) 3.200% 2046	2.3	6-Jul-21
Philippines (Sovereign) 2.95% 2045	1.4	5-May-20	Philippines (Sovereign) 1.375% 2026	1.1	8-Oct-21
Others	12.6		Others	7.5	
Singapore	14.7		Singapore	16.5	
United Overseas Bank 0.010% 2027	1.2	1-Dec-20	BOC Aviation 1.625% 2024	1.0	29-Apr-21
Oversea-Chinese Banking Corporation 1.832% 2030	1.0	10-Sep-20	Temasek Financial I 2.750% 2061	1.0	2-Aug-21
Others	12.5		Others	14.5	
Thailand	5.3		Thailand	4.1	
Bangkok Bank in Hong Kong, China 5.0% Perpetual	0.8	23-Sep-20	Bankok Bank in Hong Kong, China 3.466% 2036	1.0	23-Sep-21
PTT Treasury 3.7% 2070	0.7	16-Jul-20	GC Treasury Center 2.980% 2031	0.7	18-Mar-21
Others	3.8		Others	2.4	
Viet Nam	0.1		Viet Nam	1.6	
Emerging East Asia Total	378.1		Emerging East Asia Total	376.4	
Memo Items:			Memo Items:		
India	14.3		India	23.7	
Vedanta Holdings Mauritius II 13.00% 2023	1.4	21-Aug-20	Vedanta Resources 8.95% 2025	1.2	11-Mar-21
Others	12.9		Others	22.5	
Sri Lanka	0.4		Sri Lanka	0.8	
Sri Lanka (Sovereign) 6.57% 2021	0.1	30-Jul-20	Sri Lanka (Sovereign) 7.95% 2024	0.2	3-May-21
Others	0.3		Others	0.6	

USD = United States dollar.
Notes:
1. Data exclude certificates of deposit.
2. G3 currency bonds are bonds denominated in either euros, Japanese yen, or US dollars.
3. Bloomberg LP end-of-period rates are used.
4. Emerging East Asia comprises Cambodia; the People's Republic of China; Hong Kong, China; Indonesia; the Republic of Korea; Malaysia; the Philippines; Singapore; Thailand; and Viet Nam.
5. Figures after the issuer name reflect the coupon rate and year of maturity of the bond.
Source: *AsianBondsOnline* calculations based on Bloomberg LP data.

covered bond in October. Proceeds from the issuance will be used to fund green and social projects of the company.

Hong Kong, China accounted for a 10.5% share of all bonds denominated in G3 currencies in 2021. This comprised USD-denominated bonds that amounted to USD36.5 billion, while a total of USD2.9 billion was EUR-denominated, and bonds denominated in Japanese yen amounted to USD0.3 billion. In November, the government raised USD3.0 billion from its multicurrency green bond issuance: the EUR-denominated tranches had tenors of 5 years and 20 years, while the USD-denominated tranche had a maturity of 10 years. Funds raised from the issuance will be part of Hong Kong, China's Capital Works Reserve Fund, which will be used for sustainable economic development projects. The issuance is also meant to expand Hong Kong, China's investor base. The Hong Kong Mortgage Corporation, a government-owned entity, offered 10 USD-denominated bond issuances in Q4 2021 amounting to USD550.0 million and with tenors from 1 year to 3 years.

G3 currency bonds issued by ASEAN member economies in 2021 dropped 7.0% y-o-y.[5] G3 currency bond issuance in the region totaled USD75.4 billion, which was down from the USD81.0 billion issued in 2020, as fund-raising activities in most economies slowed during the year. Only Singapore and Viet Nam posted increased issuance of G3 currency bonds in 2021. ASEAN issuance in 2021 was at 20.0% of total G3 currency bond issuance in emerging East Asia, less than the 21.4% share recorded in 2020. During the review period, Indonesia continued to have the highest volume of G3 currency bond issuance in the ASEAN region despite the decline in its issuance. Singapore, Malaysia, the Philippines, Thailand, and Viet Nam followed in descending order in terms of issuance volume.

In 2021, G3 currency bond issuances in Indonesia accounted for 7.0% of the total in emerging East Asia at USD23.3 billion in US dollars, USD2.3 billion equivalent in euros, and USD0.9 billion equivalent in Japanese yen. Bank Indonesia raised about USD1.4 billion in short-term, zero-coupon USD-denominated securities in Q4 2021 as part of the government's stimulus program to combat the effects of the COVID-19 pandemic. In October, Indofood CBP, a producer of consumer products, issued a USD1.0 billion dual-tranche USD-denominated global

bond with tenors of 11 years and 31 years. Proceeds from the issuance will be used to meet the company's obligations in its acquisition of Pinehill Company and for general corporate purposes.

Singapore accounted for 4.4% of total G3 currency bonds issued in emerging East Asia in 2021 with USD13.6 billion in US dollars, USD2.5 billion equivalent in euros, and USD0.4 billion equivalent in Japanese yen. In October, DBS Bank expanded its stock of G3 currency bonds by issuing a dual-currency bond: a EUR-denominated tranche worth USD852.8 million and a USD-denominated tranche amounting to USD210.0 million. Both tranches had a tenor of 5 years. In December, real estate company Mapletree Logistics Trust issued two samurai bonds. The first one was an 8-year bond equivalent to USD17.4 million and with a coupon rate of 0.7%. The second issuance was a dual-tranche bond totaling USD104.3 million, both of which had a tenor of 9 years and a coupon rate of 0.9%. Proceeds from the latest samurai bond issuance will be used for general corporate purposes and for refinancing existing obligations.

During the review period, G3 currency bonds issuance in Malaysia was 4.2% of the total for emerging East Asia with USD-denominated issuances totaling USD15.9 billion and JPY-denominated bonds amounting to USD0.1 billion. In October, Malayan Banking increased its stock of USD-denominated and JPY-denominated bonds through separate issuances during the month. The USD-denominated bond was a USD255.0 million zero-coupon bond with a tenor of 40 years, while the samurai bond was a 5-year bond totaling USD86.9 million and with a coupon rate of 0.21%. In November, the Export–Import Bank of Malaysia issued a 5-year USD350.0 million USD-denominated bond with a coupon rate of 1.831%. Issued through the company's multicurrency medium-term note program, proceeds from the issuance will be used for general corporate purposes.

A 2.9% share of total issuance of G3 currency bonds in emerging East Asia in 2021 came from the Philippines. In terms of currency, US dollar bonds totaled USD8.0 billion, USD2.4 billion worth of bonds were denominated in euros, and JPY-denominated bonds totaled USD0.5 billion. In October, the Government of the Philippines issued a USD1.6 billion dual-tranche USD-denominated retail onshore dollar bonds with maturities of 5 years and

---

[5] For the discussion on G3 currency issuance, data for ASEAN include Cambodia, Indonesia, Malaysia, the Philippines, Singapore, Thailand, and Viet Nam.

10 years. The issuance aimed to attract retail investors to foster a more inclusive investment environment in the Philippines. In November, Globe Telecommunications raised USD600.0 million from its issuance of a USD-denominated perpetual bond with a 4.2% coupon rate. Proceeds from the offering will be used for the telecommunications company's capital expenditures, the refinancing of existing debts, and other general corporate purposes.

During the review period, Thailand had a share of 1.1% of all G3 currency bonds issued in the region, raising funds solely in US dollars totaling USD4.1 billion. In October, life insurance company Muang Thai Life Assurance issued a 15-year USD-denominated callable bond with a coupon rate of 3.552%. The USD400 million raised from the offering will be used for general corporate purposes and to meet capital requirements.

Only 0.4% of all G3 currency bonds issued in emerging East Asia were from Viet Nam in 2021, with USD-denominated bonds worth USD1.6 billion. In December, property developer Phu My Hung Development raised USD150.0 million from a 5-year USD-denominated bond. The bond had a coupon rate of 2.0% and proceeds will be part of the company's guarantee facility.

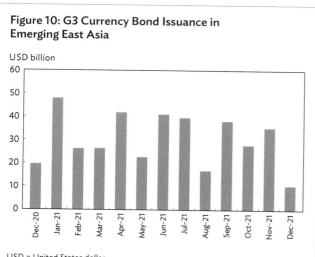

Figure 10: G3 Currency Bond Issuance in Emerging East Asia

USD billion

USD = United States dollar.
Notes:
1. Emerging East Asia comprises Cambodia; the People's Republic of China; Hong Kong, China; Indonesia; the Republic of Korea; the Lao People's Democratic Republic; Malaysia; the Philippines; Singapore; Thailand; and Viet Nam.
2. G3 currency bonds are bonds denominated in either euros, Japanese yen, or US dollars.
3. Figures were computed based on 31 December 2021 currency exchange rates and do not include currency effects.
Source: *AsianBondsOnline* calculations based on Bloomberg LP data.

Emerging East Asia's monthly G3 currency bond issuance from December 2020 to December 2021 is shown in **Figure 10**. After a dip in October, issuance picked up again in November as most economies ramped up their G3 currency fund-raising activities. Issuance fell again across all economies in the region in December as the Omicron variant of COVID-19 caused concerns around the world, and as markets anticipated a further reduction in the US Federal Reserve's asset purchases. The low December issuance volume resulted in less G3 currency bond issuance in 2021 than in 2020.

Bond Yield Movements

Emerging East Asia's government bond yields rose as central banks globally began tightening monetary policy in response to rising inflation.

As economies continue to recover, global inflation has begun to rise, prompting many central banks and monetary authorities to begin tightening monetary policy. The Federal Reserve announced during its 2–3 November meeting that it would begin reducing the pace of its monthly asset purchases by USD10 billion for US Treasuries and USD5 billion for mortgage-backed securities each month. The Federal Reserve later accelerated the pace of its monthly reductions to USD20 billion and USD10 billion, respectively, at its 14–15 December meeting, with its asset purchases set to end entirely in March 2022. Further tightening was also done during its 15-16 March meeting, where it raised the Federal funds target rate range by 25 basis points (bps) to 0.25% to 0.50%. The Federal Reserve also said that it could also begin reducing its bond holdings in an upcoming meeting.

The European Central Bank (ECB) has also slowed the pace of its asset purchases, with the amounts purchased under the Pandemic Emergency Purchase Programme (PEPP) being reduced each quarter. During its 16 December meeting, the ECB affirmed that the PEPP would end in March 2022. However, there would be a transition period wherein after the end of the PEPP, monthly purchases under the Asset Purchase Programme (APP) would be increased to EUR40 billion in Q2 2022 before falling to EUR30 billion in Q3 2022 and EUR20 billion in successive quarters. The ECB provided no indication when the APP was set to end but did mention that a rate hike was unlikely. However, in the ECB's 3 February meeting, the ECB noted that inflation was running higher than previously expected, and it subsequently refrained from saying that a rate hike was unlikely. During its 10 March meeting, the ECB announced that it would accelerate the reduction of its APP to EUR40 billion in April, EUR30 billion in May, and EUR20 billion June and could stop the APP in the third quarter subject to incoming data.

The Bank of Japan (BOJ) was the furthest along among its peers in normalizing monetary policy. During its 18 January meeting, monetary policy was largely left unchanged but the BOJ affirmed that purchases of commercial paper and corporate bonds would end in March 2022, but purchases of Japanese Government Bonds would continue. The BOJ also said that its policy rates are expected to remain at current levels or below, suggesting that economic conditions did not yet warrant discussion on the timing of rate adjustments.

Among other advanced economies, the Bank of England (BOE) has also been tightening in response to rising inflation. On 16 December, the BOE raised the base rate to 0.25% from 0.10%. On 3 February, the BOE raised the base rate by an additional 25 bps to 0.50%.

Yields have also risen in emerging East Asia, pressured by central banks in advanced economies and the region. The 2-year yield trended upward in nearly all emerging East Asian markets between 30 November 2021 and 15 February 2022. A strong rise in 2-year yields was seen in the Republic of Korea and Hong Kong, China (**Figure 11a**). In particular, the Republic of Korea had

the largest gain in the 2-year yield among emerging East Asian markets following the Bank of Korea's efforts to rein in inflation. In contrast, Hong Kong, China's rise in yields followed US yields, owing to the economy's lack of independent monetary policy.

The PRC was the sole market in emerging East Asia to show a noticeable decline in its 2-year yield, as the slowing economy necessitated additional support from the People's Bank of China (PBOC). The Philippines' 2-year yield declined from the start of December through the first half of January due to ample liquidity in the banking system, but the yield began rising following indications that the Federal Reserve would raise interest rates at its next monetary meeting in March (**Figure 11b**). Thailand's 2-year yield was roughly stable during the review period, exhibiting only a mild decline.

Emerging East Asia's 10-year yields largely followed similar patterns to those of the 2-year yields. The steepest rise among 10-year yields was again noted in the Republic of Korea (**Figure 12a**). Hong Kong, China's and Singapore's 10-year yields also mirrored movements in their respective 2-year yields. Bucking the regional trend once again, the PRC's 10-year yield exhibited a notable decline.

In contrast to the movement in its 2-year yield, Thailand's 10-year yield rose during the review period (**Figure 12b**). The Philippines' 10-year yield followed a similar pattern to its 2-year yield, but the spike in its 10-year yield toward the end of the review period was significantly higher.

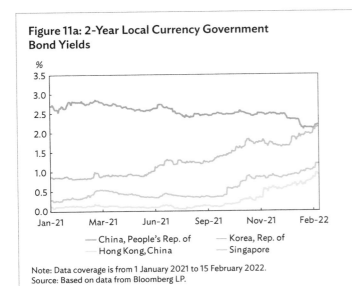

Figure 11a: 2-Year Local Currency Government Bond Yields

Note: Data coverage is from 1 January 2021 to 15 February 2022.
Source: Based on data from Bloomberg LP.

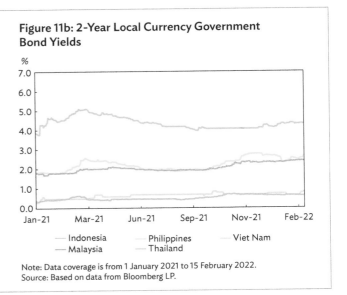

Figure 11b: 2-Year Local Currency Government Bond Yields

Note: Data coverage is from 1 January 2021 to 15 February 2022.
Source: Based on data from Bloomberg LP.

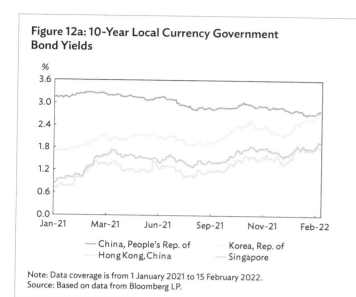

Figure 12a: 10-Year Local Currency Government Bond Yields

Note: Data coverage is from 1 January 2021 to 15 February 2022.
Source: Based on data from Bloomberg LP.

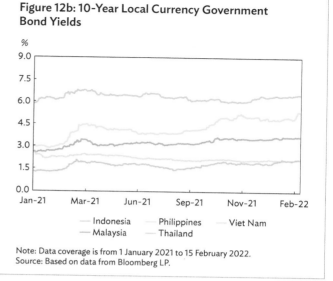

Figure 12b: 10-Year Local Currency Government Bond Yields

Note: Data coverage is from 1 January 2021 to 15 February 2022.
Source: Based on data from Bloomberg LP.

Yield curve movements in emerging East Asia followed trends in the 2-year and 10-year yields, with all markets except the PRC showing a rising yield curve between 30 November and 15 February (**Figure 13**). The most pronounced upward shift was in the Republic of Korea, where the yield curve shifted upward by an average of 39 bps across all tenors. The yield curves of Hong Kong, China and Singapore also rose across all tenors by an average of 27 bps and 24 bps, respectively. All other regional markets except the PRC showed a rise in most tenors across the yield curve.

In the Philippines and Thailand, there was a decline in yields with tenors of 2 years or less, reflecting abundant liquidity in the financial system with many banks preferring shorter-term tenors in expectation of higher interest rates.

The 2-year versus 10-year yield rose in all markets except in Hong Kong, China; the Republic of Korea; Singapore; and Viet Nam (**Figure 14**).

The PRC was the only market in emerging East Asia to exhibit a notable decline in its yields, largely due to the weakening of its economic growth and concerns regarding property company defaults. The PRC's GDP growth slowed to 4.0% y-o-y in Q4 2021 from 4.9% y-o-y in Q3 2021 and 7.9% y-o-y in Q2 2021. Similarly, Hong Kong, China's GDP growth slowed to 4.8% y-o-y in Q4 2021 from 5.5% y-o-y in Q3 2021. Singapore's

GPP growth also slowed to 6.1% y-o-y in Q4 2021 from 7.5.% y-o-y in Q3 2021.

In contrast, other markets in the region experienced a quickening in their GDP growth in Q4 2021 as economies begin to recover from the pandemic and gradually open up. The fastest recovery of Q4 2021 was in Viet Nam, where GDP bounced back with growth of 5.2% y-o-y in Q4 2021 from a decline of 6.2% y-o-y in the previous quarter. Malaysia's GDP also recovered in Q4 2021 with growth of 3.6% y-o-y following a 4.5% y-o-y contraction in the previous quarter. In addition, Thailand reported positive GDP growth of 1.9% y-o-y in Q4 2021 after a 0.2% y-o-y decline in Q3 2021. Both Indonesia and the Philippines reported slightly better GDP growth results in Q4 2021 at 5.0% y-o-y and 7.7% y-o-y, respectively, versus 3.5% y-o-y and 6.9% y-o-y in Q3 2021. The Republic of Korea had roughly stable GDP growth in Q4 2021 at 4.2% y-o-y versus 4.0% y-o-y in Q3 2021.

With economic recovery underway in most markets, inflation in the region has been trending upward. Among all economies in the region, Singapore had the highest inflation rate at the end of January (**Figure 15a**). After recording the highest inflation rate in the region in Q3 2021, inflation in the Philippines trended downward in Q4 2021 (**Figure 15b**).

With inflation on the rise, some central banks and monetary authorities in emerging East Asia have begun

Figure 13: Benchmark Yield Curves—Local Currency Government Bonds

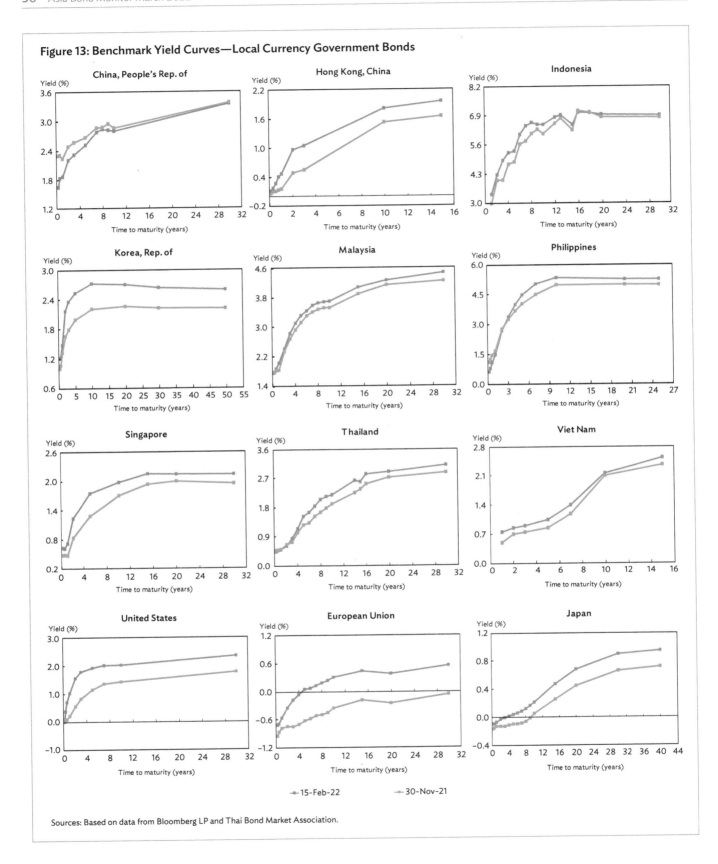

Sources: Based on data from Bloomberg LP and Thai Bond Market Association.

tightening. The first to do so was the Bank of Korea beginning with a rate increase on 26 August 2021 and continuing on 25 November 2021 and again on 14 January 2022 (**Table 5**). Monetary Authority of Singapore twice raised the slope of its Singapore Dollar Nominal Effective Exchange Rate, the first time on 14 October 2021 and again on 25 January 2022 in an off-schedule meeting.

While some central banks in emerging East Asia were tightening, the PBOC had the distinction of being the only regional central bank to ease monetary policy. The PBOC reduced by 50 bps the reserve requirement ratio on 6 December. It also reduced by 10 bps the rate on its 1-year medium-term lending facility to 2.85% on 16 January.

Corporate spreads largely rose in the PRC and the Republic of Korea.

The spread between AAA-rated yields and government yields rose in the PRC and the Republic of Korea. In the PRC, demand for AAA-rated paper fell amid rising credit concerns and the potential spillover from defaults in the property sector. In the Republic of Korea, spreads widened largely due to concerns of a slowdown as the Bank of Korea tightened monetary policy. The spread fell in Malaysia on a return to GDP growth in Q4 2021 and was unchanged in Thailand (**Figure 16a**).

For lower-rated bonds, spreads were unchanged in most markets for which data are available but rose in Malaysia. (**Figure 16b**).

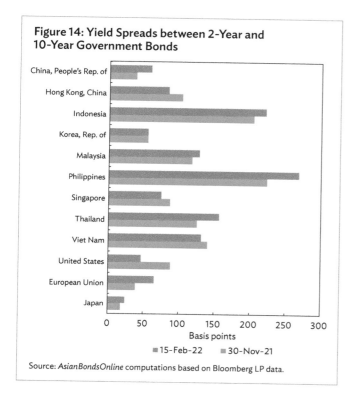

Figure 14: Yield Spreads between 2-Year and 10-Year Government Bonds

Source: *AsianBondsOnline* computations based on Bloomberg LP data.

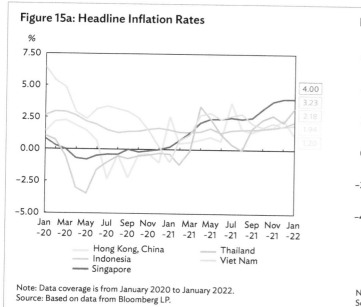

Figure 15a: Headline Inflation Rates

Note: Data coverage is from January 2020 to January 2022.
Source: Based on data from Bloomberg LP.

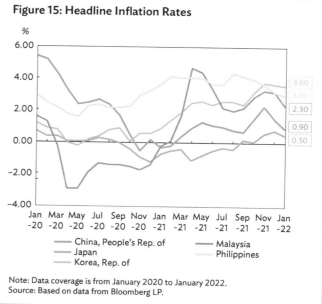

Figure 15: Headline Inflation Rates

Note: Data coverage is from January 2020 to January 2022.
Source: Based on data from Bloomberg LP.

Table 5: Policy Rate Changes

Economy	Policy Rate 31-Jan-2021 (%)	Rate Change (%)													Policy Rate 15-Feb-2022 (%)	Change in Policy Rates (basis points)
		Feb-2021	Mar-2021	Apr-2021	May-2021	Jun-2021	Jul-2021	Aug-2021	Sep-2021	Oct-2021	Nov-2021	Dec-2021	Jan-2022	Feb-2022		
United States	0.25														0.25	0
Euro Area	(0.50)														(0.50)	0
Japan	(0.10)														(0.10)	0
China, People's Rep. of	2.95												↓0.10		2.85	↓ 10
Indonesia	3.75	↓0.25													3.50	↓ 25
Korea, Rep. of	0.50							↑0.25			↑0.25		↑0.25		1.25	↑ 75
Malaysia	1.75														1.75	0
Philippines	2.00														2.00	0
Singapore	–									↑			↑		–	–
Thailand	0.50														0.50	0
Viet Nam	4.00														4.00	0

( ) = negative.
Notes:
1. Data coverage is from 31 January 2021 to 15 February 2022.
2. For the People's Republic of China, data used in the chart are for the 1-year medium-term lending facility rate. While the 1-year benchmark lending rate is the official policy rate of the People's Bank of China, market players use the 1-year medium-term lending facility rate as a guide for the monetary policy direction of the People's Bank of China.
3. The up (down) arrow for Singapore signifies monetary policy tightening (loosening) by its central bank. Monetary Authority of Singapore utilizes the exchange rate to guide its monetary policy.
Sources: Various central bank websites.

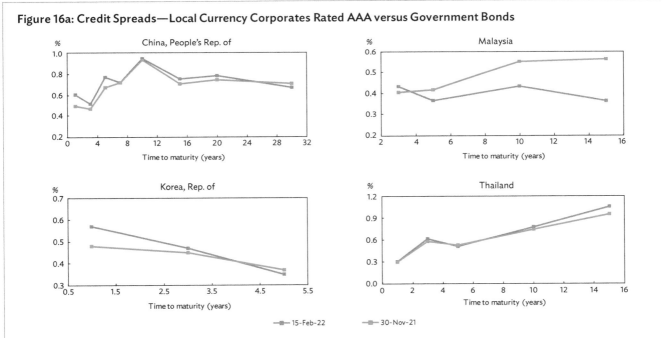

Figure 16a: Credit Spreads—Local Currency Corporates Rated AAA versus Government Bonds

Notes:
1. Credit spreads are obtained by subtracting government yields from corporate indicative yields.
2. For Malaysia, data on corporate bond yields are as of 30 November 2021 and 14 February 2022.
Sources: People's Republic of China (Bloomberg LP); Republic of Korea (KG Zeroin Corporation); Malaysia (Fully Automated System for Issuing/Tendering Bank Negara Malaysia); and Thailand (Bloomberg LP).

Figure 16b: Credit Spreads—Lower-Rated Local Currency Corporates versus AAA

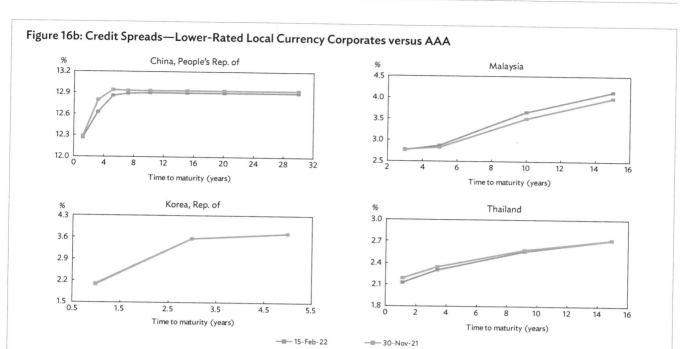

Notes:
1. Credit spreads are obtained by subtracting government yields from corporate indicative yields.
2. For Malaysia, data on corporate bond yields are as of 30 November 2021 and 14 February 2022.
Sources: People's Republic of China (Bloomberg LP); Republic of Korea (KG Zeroin Corporation); Malaysia (Fully Automated System for Issuing/Tendering Bank Negara Malaysia); and Thailand (Bloomberg LP).

Recent Developments in ASEAN+3 Sustainable Bond Markets

Sustainable bond markets in ASEAN+3 continued to expand rapidly in 2021 amid rising interest in and awareness of environmental, social, and governance (ESG) investments.[6] The amount of outstanding sustainable bonds—which comprise green, social, sustainable, sustainability-linked, and transition bonds—climbed to USD430.7 billion at the end of December 2021 (**Figure 17**). This was up from USD409.7 billion at the end of September and reflected a more than 50% annual increase from USD274.1 billion at the end of December 2020. While green bonds continued to dominate the ASEAN+3 sustainable bond market, accounting for 68.2% of the regional total, interest in other types of sustainable bonds has been rising. The

shares of social and sustainability bonds increased to 13.5% and 14.7%, respectively, from 11.5% and 11.7% at the end of 2020. Despite their respective shares remaining low, sustainability-linked bonds and transition bonds outstanding also expanded in size in 2021 amid their nascent stage of market development.

ASEAN+3 sustainable bonds accounted for 18.3% of the global market of USD2,352.0 billion at the end of Q4 2021, making it the world's second-largest regional sustainable bond market (**Figure 18**). Europe remained the world's largest regional sustainable bond market, accounting for 49.2% of the global total. Among sustainable bond types, ASEAN+3 is home to the

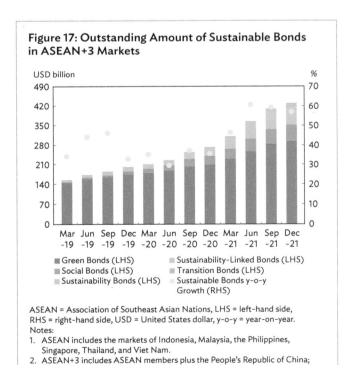

Figure 17: Outstanding Amount of Sustainable Bonds in ASEAN+3 Markets

ASEAN = Association of Southeast Asian Nations, LHS = left-hand side, RHS = right-hand side, USD = United States dollar, y-o-y = year-on-year.
Notes:
1. ASEAN includes the markets of Indonesia, Malaysia, the Philippines, Singapore, Thailand, and Viet Nam.
2. ASEAN+3 includes ASEAN members plus the People's Republic of China; Hong Kong, China; Japan; and the Republic of Korea.
3. Data include both local currency and foreign currency issues.
Source: *AsianBondsOnline* computations based on Bloomberg LP data.

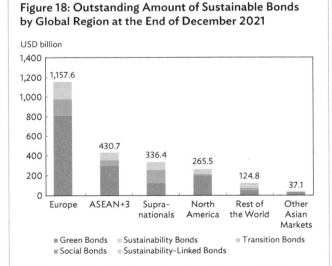

Figure 18: Outstanding Amount of Sustainable Bonds by Global Region at the End of December 2021

ASEAN = Association of Southeast Asian Nations, USD = United States dollar.
Notes:
1. ASEAN includes the markets of Indonesia, Malaysia, the Philippines, Singapore, Thailand, and Viet Nam.
2. ASEAN+3 includes ASEAN members plus the People's Republic of China; Hong Kong, China; Japan; and the Republic of Korea.
3. Data include both local currency and foreign currency issues.
Source: *AsianBondsOnline* computations based on Bloomberg LP data.

---

[6] For the discussion on sustainable bonds, ASEAN+3 includes Association of Southeast Asian Nations (ASEAN) members Indonesia, Malaysia, the Philippines, Singapore, Thailand, and Viet Nam plus the People's Republic of China; Hong Kong, China; Japan; and the Republic of Korea.

largest transition bond market in the world at a size of USD3.2 billion, representing 52.3% of transition bonds outstanding globally.

More diversified market profiles were observed for each bond type in 2021 compared to 2020 (**Figure 19**). The People's Republic of China (PRC) continued to dominate the ASEAN+3 green bond market, accounting for 65.2% of the regional green bond total in 2021. ASEAN markets contributed a slightly higher share of 5.9% in 2021 compared to 5.8% in 2020. Social bonds outstanding in the region expanded to USD58.1 billion at the end of 2021, dominated by the Republic of Korea and Japan, which accounted for 60.7% and 37.1% of the regional total, respectively. By the end of December 2021, regional sustainability bonds climbed to USD63.5 billion. Similar to the end of 2020, the Republic of Korea and Japan accounted for a combined 70.5% market share. Meanwhile, ASEAN accounted for a 17.1% share, while the PRC's share increased from 7.8% to 11.5% during the review period. Sustainability-linked bonds outstanding were USD12.3 billion at the end of December 2021, with

the PRC's share increasing significantly to 64.1% from 46.8% a year earlier. The amount of transition bonds outstanding was the smallest among all sustainable bond types at USD3.2 billion. Issuers of transition bonds were largely from Hong Kong, China and the PRC, with shares of 59.9% and 34.6%, respectively.

Driven by rising awareness of ESG investments, quarterly issuance of sustainable bonds in ASEAN+3 markets was robust in 2021 compared with prior years. Sustainable bond issuance reached USD239.5 billion in 2021, more than double the 2020 level of USD96.1 billion. In the fourth quarter of 2021, total issuance reached USD58.0 billion on 120.9% year-on-year growth (**Figure 20**). Among the different bond types, green bonds remained the most popular sustainable bond due to increasing concern about climate change. The share of green bonds to total sustainable bond issuance rose to 65.6% in 2021 from 60.0% in 2020. Sustainability-linked bonds also generated greater investor interest in 2021, with their share of sustainable bond issuance in ASEAN+3 climbing to 4.9% from 0.3% in 2020.

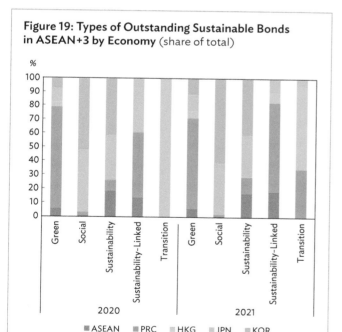

Figure 19: Types of Outstanding Sustainable Bonds in ASEAN+3 by Economy (share of total)

ASEAN = Association of Southeast Asian Nations; PRC = People's Republic of China; HKG = Hong Kong, China; JPN = Japan; KOR = Republic of Korea.
Notes:
1. ASEAN includes the markets of Indonesia, Malaysia, the Philippines, Singapore, Thailand, and Viet Nam.
2. ASEAN+3 includes ASEAN members plus the People's Republic of China; Hong Kong, China; Japan; and the Republic of Korea.
3. Data include both local currency and foreign currency issues.
Source: *AsianBondsOnline* computations based on Bloomberg LP data.

Figure 20: Quarterly Issuance Volume of Sustainable Bonds in ASEAN+3 Markets

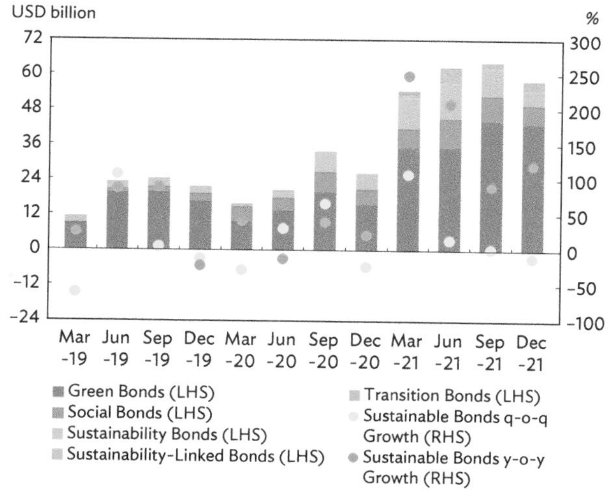

ASEAN = Association of Southeast Asian Nations, LHS = left-hand side, q-o-q = quarter-on-quarter, RHS = right-hand side, USD = United States dollar, y-o-y = year-on-year.
Notes:
1. ASEAN includes the markets of Indonesia, Malaysia, the Philippines, Singapore, Thailand, and Viet Nam.
2. ASEAN+3 includes ASEAN members plus the People's Republic of China; Hong Kong, China; Japan; and the Republic of Korea.
3. Data include both local currency and foreign currency issues.
Source: *AsianBondsOnline* computations based on Bloomberg LP data.

Private sector issuers dominated sustainable bond issuance in the region in 2021, with all bond types benefiting from a more diversified issuer profile compared with the previous year (**Figure 21**). The financial sector was the primary issuer of sustainable bonds in ASEAN+3 markets in 2021, especially in the social bond and sustainability bond markets. While investor interest in sustainable bonds rose in 2021, demand was largely for shorter-term financing: 50.7% of sustainable bond issuance in 2021 comprised bonds with maturities of 5 years or less (**Figure 22**). The majority of green bonds (52.7%) and social bonds (57.8%) issued in 2021 had tenors of 5 years or less, while the majority of sustainability bonds (62.6%) and transition bonds (52.7%) issued in 2021 had tenors of more than 5 years. Further, the share of local currency sustainable bonds decreased to 61.5% in 2021 from 68.2% in 2020. Local currency issuance was largely seen in green, social, and sustainability-linked bond issuances, while more foreign currency bond issuance was observed in sustainability and transition bonds.

Information asymmetry and transparency is a critical development issue in the sustainable bond market. Evidence shows that green bonds, particularly those with green labels and certifications, tend to benefit from a negative green premium compared to similar conventional bonds. **Box 3** provides additional evidence

to show that frequent green bond issuers also enjoy cost benefits due to reduced information asymmetry. **Box 4** summarizes market participants' views on the importance of integrity and transparency in ESG investments.

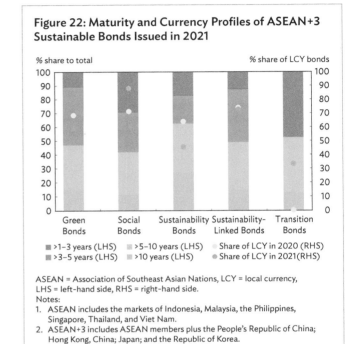

Figure 22: Maturity and Currency Profiles of ASEAN+3 Sustainable Bonds Issued in 2021

ASEAN = Association of Southeast Asian Nations, LCY = local currency, LHS = left-hand side, RHS = right-hand side.
Notes:
1. ASEAN includes the markets of Indonesia, Malaysia, the Philippines, Singapore, Thailand, and Viet Nam.
2. ASEAN+3 includes ASEAN members plus the People's Republic of China; Hong Kong, China; Japan; and the Republic of Korea.
3. Data include both local currency and foreign currency issues.
Source: *AsianBondsOnline* computations based on Bloomberg LP data.

Figure 21: Issuance of Sustainable Bonds in ASEAN+3 by Sector (% share of total)

ASEAN = Association of Southeast Asian Nations.
Notes:
1. ASEAN includes the markets of Indonesia, Malaysia, the Philippines, Singapore, Thailand, and Viet Nam.
2. ASEAN+3 includes ASEAN members plus the People's Republic of China; Hong Kong, China; Japan; and the Republic of Korea.
3. Data include both foreign currency and local currency issues.
Source: *AsianBondsOnline* computations based on Bloomberg LP data.

Box 3: Pricing of Frequent Green Bond Issuance

In recent years, green bonds have become a widely adopted instrument to finance projects with positive environmental impacts.[a] A well-functioning green bond market helps to channel capital from both the public and private sectors to green investments, while reducing financing costs and fostering risk-sharing.

The financial markets have priced in climate-change-related risks as awareness of the risks associated with climate change increases, which has boosted the supply of and demand for green bonds worldwide. On the supply side, issuing green bonds can save funding costs, build social capital by strengthening an issuer's reputation with stakeholders, gain positive investor recognition, and attract a more diversified investor base. On the demand side, investing in green bonds helps stabilize capital inflows, build greater resilience during market turmoil, and provide hedging and diversification benefits (Climate Bonds Initiative 2021, Asian Development Bank 2021). Annual global green bond issuance increased from USD70.1 billion in 2014 to USD596.6 billion in 2021 (**Figure B3.1**).

Nevertheless, the green bond market's development still faces key challenges. One of the most pronounced challenges is the information asymmetry associated with environmental performance, which directly links to possible greenwashing-related reputational risks and undermines investor confidence. Shapiro (2021) reviewed green bonds listed in the Climate Bonds Database issued between November 2017 and

March 2019 and found that only 77% of green bond issuers published information on the allocation of proceeds and only 59% quantified the environmental impact of the financed projects. Demand for greater transparency and integrity on the use of green bond proceeds has grown in parallel with the rapid expansion of the green bond market. **Figure B3.2** depicts how often people are searching for the terms "green bonds" and "greenwashing" on Google.

To boost information disclosure, policy makers and the investment community are seeking to define a clear taxonomy and market standards, and are introducing information-enhancing mechanisms—such as external verification, certification, and labels—as part of the green bond market ecosystem to mitigate information asymmetry and reputational risks. These information-enhancing practices can reduce funding costs for reliable green bonds through greater information transparency and lower reputational risks (Hyun, Park, and Tian 2020) However, such benefits are partly offset by the additional cost associated with related services.

This study explores a new and cost-efficient mechanism that helps reduce information asymmetry and reputational risks: frequent green bond issuance. By repeatedly tapping the green bond market to finance green investments, frequent bond issuers can recycle existing knowledge,

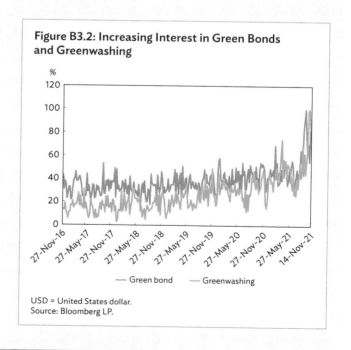

Figure B3.1: Global Green Bond Issuance

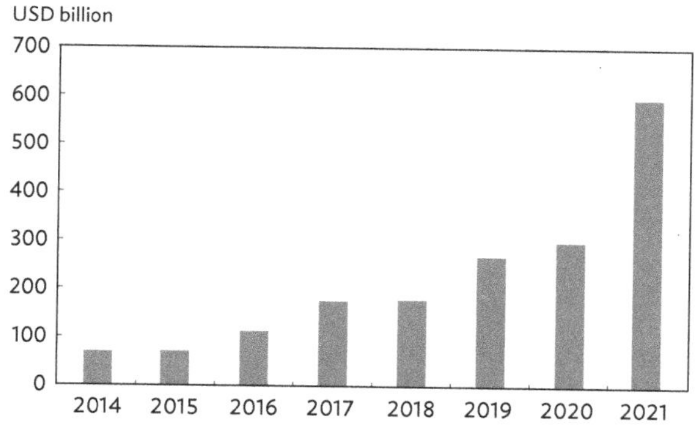

USD = United States dollar.
Source: Bloomberg LP.

Figure B3.2: Increasing Interest in Green Bonds and Greenwashing

USD = United States dollar.
Source: Bloomberg LP.

[a] This box was written by Suk Hyun, Donghyun Park, and Shu Tian and is based on Hyun, S., D. Park, and S. Tian. 2022. "The Price of Frequent Issuance: Value of Information in the Green Bond Market." Yonsei University Working Paper.

Box 3 *continued*

capacity, and market relationships in any subsequent green bond issuance, reducing the marginal costs of an additional green bond issuance. Regardless of third-party assessment, frequent green bond issuers have conducted more reporting on and monitoring of green bond proceeds, which provides more information on an issuer's reliability relative to new or infrequent green bond issuers. Moreover, by frequently issuing green bonds, issuers also signal a stronger environmental commitment by persistently investing in green projects (Flammer 2021). Together, a strong environmental commitment and greater information transparency will help frequent issuers gain the confidence of investors, thus lowering financing costs.

Exploring global green bond issuance data from Bloomberg from 2014 to 2019, this study utilizes the Oaxaca–Blinder decomposition approach to determine to what extent common bond pricing factors—such as issuance size, credit rating, maturity, coupon rate, liquidity, and green label—help explain the yield difference between frequent and infrequent green bond issuers, and to what extent the unobserved factors beyond existing bond pricing can explain the yield difference. As the yield difference reflects whether an issuer frequently taps the green bond market, the yield difference that is unexplained by existing common pricing factors can partly reflect how the green bond market prices frequent issuance and related informational value.

Empirical evidence shows that, on average, infrequent green bond issuers pay 114–177 basis points more on their bond issuance relative to frequent green bond issuers, which can be attributed to existing green bond pricing factors such as maturity, credit rating, liquidity, and green label. More importantly, the evidence reports an 8-basis-points bond yield difference between frequent and infrequent issuers that cannot be explained by the aforementioned common bond pricing factors. This yield difference thus captures some additional pricing mechanism between frequent and infrequent issuers, as frequent issuers tend to have

greater information transparency that is already priced in by potential investors.

These new findings offer useful policy implications. While it is important to further develop the green bond market ecosystem and reduce information asymmetry via disclosure requirements, information-enhancing financial services, intermediaries, and policy makers should encourage existing green bond issuers to continue issuing green bonds. Frequent green bond issuance not only lowers investor information asymmetry, thereby boosting investor confidence, but it also reduces issuer financing costs in a relatively cost-efficient manner. From a market development perspective, encouraging frequent green bond issuance can boost the supply of and demand for green bonds, benefiting market depth and liquidity. Further research into the knowledge-identifying factors that affect the decisions of frequent green bond issuers could provide useful policy implications on how to encourage frequent green bond issuances.

References

Asian Development Bank. 2021. *Asian Development Outlook 2021: Financing a Green and Inclusive Recovery*. https://www.adb.org/sites/default/files/publication/692111/ado2021-theme-chapter.pdf.

Climate Bonds Initiative. 2021. *Green Bond Pricing in the Primary Market H1 2021, September 2021. Greenium Persists in H1 202—plus Latest Research Reflects Ongoing Green Bond Pricing Benefits for Investors.* https://www.climatebonds.net/resources/press-releases/2021/09/greenium-persists-h1-2021-plus-latest-research-reflects-ongoing.

Hyun, Suk, Donghyun Park, and Shu Tian. 2020. "The Price of Going Green: The Role of Greenness in Green Bond Markets." *Accounting & Finance* 60 (1): 73–95.

Flammer, Caroline. 2021. "Corporate Green Bonds." *Journal of Financial Economics* 142 (2): 499–516.

Shapiro, Lori. 2021. "Are Greenwashing Fears Overstated?" *S&P Global Rating*. 23 August.

Box 4: Asian Development Bank–State Street Global Advisors Webinar Series— Progress toward Greater Sustainable Market Efficiency and Integrity

In late 2021, the Asian Development Bank (ADB) and State Street Global Advisors collaborated to host a three-part webinar series, Asia's Progress toward Greater Sustainable Financial Market Efficiency and Integrity.[a] In this series, market participants from Asia and Europe discussed the development of sustainable taxonomies; the trend of environmental, social, and governance (ESG) centricity; and the importance of corporate climate and sustainability disclosure.

The discussions revealed insights for corporates and investors seeking to understand key trends in ESG investing, corporate disclosure, green taxonomy development, green and transition finance, and opportunities in Sustainable Development Goal (SDG)-aligned business. Speakers presented honest assessments of challenges, including the lack of sustainability disclosure standards, insufficient ESG data availability and comparability, and the tradeoffs and pitfalls encountered in ESG investing. In terms of next steps and policy recommendations, investors indicated the need for more climate-related financial disclosure such as Task Force on Climate-Related Financial Disclosures (TCFD) reporting, the development of centralized ESG databases in Asia, and credible mechanisms for channeling finance to transition- and SDG-aligned projects.

Trends and Opportunities

First, "green as an opportunity" is not just a feel-good catchphrase but an enormous mega-trend. The development of green taxonomies is not a faraway European project but one that Asian policy makers are actively shaping to finance climate change adaptation and transition in the region. Efforts are underway to align green taxonomies between Europe and the People's Republic of China to promote sustainable financial product flows. Sustainable development is a significant business opportunity: an estimated EUR270 billion and USD1.5 trillion in green and SDG-aligned investments in Europe and Asia, respectively, are required annually through 2030 (**Figure B4.1**). Meanwhile, the global total for green and other impact bonds outstanding grew to nearly USD2.2 trillion in 2021. Investors are embracing green finance, not only in recognition of the investment risks from climate change but also for the investment opportunities arising from solutions that address it.

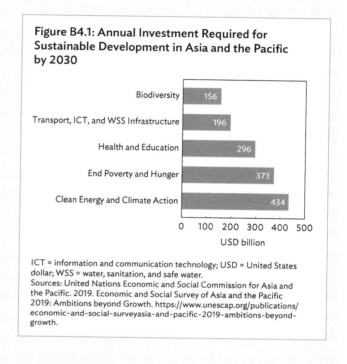

Figure B4.1: Annual Investment Required for Sustainable Development in Asia and the Pacific by 2030

ICT = information and communication technology; USD = United States dollar; WSS = water, sanitation, and safe water.
Sources: United Nations Economic and Social Commission for Asia and the Pacific. 2019. Economic and Social Survey of Asia and the Pacific 2019: Ambitions beyond Growth. https://www.unescap.org/publications/economic-and-social-surveyasia-and-pacific-2019-ambitions-beyond-growth.

Second, shifts in market preferences for sustainability and corporate transparency are fundamentally changing customer and investor decision-making, reflecting the growing centricity of ESG. Investment managers from developed markets report that 36% of total invested assets under management in their respective regions—a USD35 trillion slice of that market in 2020—is now managed according to sustainable investment principles (**Figure B4.2**). To paraphrase one of the webinar speakers: "Clients used to ask, 'why are you doing ESG investing?' Now they ask, 'Why are you not doing ESG investing?'"

Third, stakeholder accountability and business integrity is manifest in better disclosure practices by firms and the adoption of ESG investment considerations by asset owners. Corporates are finding that disclosure leads to enhanced operational awareness resulting from the inter-group coordination required to track sustainability metrics. Investors are rating companies not only by their financial performance, but also by the operational quality, governance, and strategy apparent from their disclosures. Leading firms now compete to "out-disclose" their competitors to gain a competitive edge, as this factor is increasingly a driver of investors' capital allocation decisions.

---

[a] This box was written by Jason Mortimer, head of Sustainable Investment—Fixed Income and senior portfolio manager at Nomura Asset Management.

Box 4   *continued*

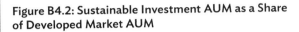

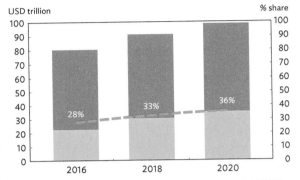

Figure B4.2: Sustainable Investment AUM as a Share of Developed Market AUM

AUM = assets under management, LHS = left-hand side, RHS = right-hand side, USD = United States dollar.
Note: Survey data include Australia, Canada, Europe, Japan, New Zealand, and the United States.
Source: Global Sustainable Investment Alliance. 2020. *Global Sustainable Investment Review.* http://www.gsi-alliance.org/wp-content/uploads/2021/08/GSIR-20201.pdf.

Challenges

Speakers pointed to a lack of standards and problems with ESG data quality and reporting consistency that makes securities analysis and investment less efficient than traditional investing. Initiatives to promote disclosure standardization such as TCFD are gaining prominence but adoption in Asia remains low. Taxonomies can help, and their development in Europe and Asia is advancing. But reaching consensus for cross-border alignment is a slow process that must account for income and development differences between jurisdictions.

Transition financing is needed to support the transition of high carbon and hard-to-abate economic sectors. But investors are often reluctant to finance these brown assets given their own net zero pledges. Asian policy makers are building transition directly into taxonomy development, and have recently announced the Energy Transition Mechanism, with ADB involvement, for enhanced credibility.

Asian investors encounter tradeoffs and unintended consequences from common ESG investment approaches. Some investors believe that negative screening and exclusion policies impose unacceptable limitations on portfolio diversification. Others described difficulties convincing some Asian companies to take disclosure and ESG compliance seriously, yet find that divestment and best-in-class ESG approaches may be irresponsible investment because investors must give up their power to positively influence companies. Overall, investors agreed that market participants must hold each other to account for maintaining integrity in sustainable finance markets.

Next Steps

Demand for sustainable investments creates a need for consistent data, measurement, labeling, and marketing by corporates and investors. This is addressable in part through promotion of industry-led standardized sustainability reporting and practical taxonomies that address transition. Investor are calling for high-quality corporate disclosure of climate-related impacts and sustainability risks and opportunities, which are now integral to their ESG investment processes. While still largely voluntary, TCFD reporting and improved sustainability performance can be promoted in Asia as a new competitive edge for corporates. Finally, investors are calling on multilateral development banks like ADB to support the creation of ESG databases and impact metrics to facilitate ESG investment integration and boost SDG- and transition-financing in emerging Asia.

Policy and Regulatory Developments

People's Republic of China

The People's Bank of China Cuts Reserve Requirement Ratio

On 6 December, the People's Bank of China reduced the reserve requirement ratio of financial institutions by 50 basis points, effective 15 December. The central bank estimates that the move will reduce the average reserve requirement ratio of financial institutions to 8.4%.

Interim Rules for Bond Connection Between Interbank and Exchange Bond Market Released

On 20 January, the Shenzhen Stock Exchange, the Shanghai Stock Exchange, the National Interbank Funding Center, Shanghai Clearing House, and China Securities Depository and Clearing Corporation jointly announced the publication of interim rules for trading between the interbank bond market and the exchange bond market. The interim rules are another step toward the interconnection of the interbank and exchange bond markets following the July 2020 announcement from the participating parties to develop such connections.

Hong Kong, China

Hong Kong Monetary Authority Issues Bond Linked to Hong Kong Overnight Index Average

On 17 November, the Hong Kong Monetary Authority (HKMA) issued its first bond indexed to the Hong Kong Overnight Index Average, an alternative to the London Interbank Offered Rate. The HKMA allocated a total of HKD1.0 billion of 1-year indexed floating-rate notes amid strong demand, receiving tender applications exceeding HKD6.4 billion.

Hong Kong Monetary Authority Continues Increase of Exchange Fund Bill Issuance

On 13 December, the HKMA announced a planned increase in issuance of 91-day Exchange Fund Bills (EFBs) by HKD5.0 billion in each of the eight regular tenders from 4 January to 22 February 2022. The HKMA had earlier increased the issuance of 91-day EFBs by HKD5.0 billion in each of the tenders from 7 September to 21 December to meet robust market demand for short-term EFBs amid abundant liquidity in the financial system.

Indonesia

Bank Indonesia Announces a Series of Upward Adjustments to the Reserve Requirement Ratio

In January, Bank Indonesia announced a series of upward adjustments to the reserve requirement ratio for conventional commercial banks, shariah banks, and shariah business units. The move was made as part of the normalization of liquidity policy. Adjustments to the reserve requirement ratio will be conducted gradually with effect on 1 March, 1 June, and 1 September. The corresponding adjustments in the rupiah reserve requirement ratio for conventional commercial banks will be from the current 3.5% to 5.0%, 6.0%, and 6.5%. For shariah banks and business units, the reserve requirement ratio will be raised from 3.5% to 4.0%, 4.5%, and 5.0%, over the same period.

Republic of Korea

National Assembly Passes the 2022 Budget

On 3 December 2021, the National Assembly passed the KRW607.7 trillion budget for 2022, which was higher than the original proposal of KRW604.4 trillion. The additions to the budget include programs intended to provide pandemic support for small businesses, boost consumption, and reinforce disease control measures. The 2022 budget was 8.9% higher than the original KRW558.0 trillion 2021 budget, and almost at par with the aggregate 2021 budget (including the two supplementary budgets) of KRW604.9 trillion. The 2022 budget is expected to result in a consolidated fiscal deficit equivalent to 2.5% of gross domestic product (GDP), an improvement from 4.4% in 2021, and a national-debt-to-GDP ratio of 50.0%, down slightly from 50.2% in 2021. The expected improvements in these two ratios were also due to an increase in the amount of revenue forecast in 2022 versus the prior year.

National Assembly Passes the First 2022 Supplementary Budget

On 21 February, the National Assembly passed the first 2022 supplementary budget worth KRW16.9 trillion, which was KRW3.3 trillion more than the original proposal. The supplementary budget is expected to provide support for small businesses and vulnerable groups, and fund disease control measures. This will bring the 2022 total budget to KRW624.3 trillion, resulting in a revised fiscal-deficit-to-GDP ratio of 3.3% versus 2.5% in the original 2022 budget.

Malaysia

Bank Negara Malaysia Establishes Business Recapitalization Facility

On 21 January, Bank Negara Malaysia established a business recapitalization facility worth MYR1.0 billion. This facility is meant to support the growth of small and medium-sized enterprises (SMEs) by providing them with financing options to manage their debt obligations. Through this facility, SMEs can obtain a combination of debt financing and equity financing from participating financial institutions, or they can obtain pure equity financing through the issuance of stocks. With the establishment of this facility, Bank Negara Malaysia also aims to help affected SMEs recover from the economic downturn caused by the pandemic.

Philippines

Bangko Sentral ng Pilipinas Expands the List of Eligible Participants to Trade Its Securities

On 10 December, the Bangko Sentral ng Pilipinas (BSP) added trust entities to the list of eligible participants to trade BSP securities in the secondary market. According to the central bank, the increase in secondary market participation is in line with BSP's continued efforts to strengthen the effectiveness of its market-based instruments for monetary operations.

Bangko Sentral ng Pilipinas Includes Digital Banks in Its Monetary Operations

On 10 December, the BSP approved the addition of digital banks to the list of eligible participants in the BSP's monetary operations to further improve the transmission of monetary policy. The inclusion will provide digital banks access to the BSP's facilities—including the reverse repurchase facility, overnight lending facility, overnight deposit facility, term deposit facility, and BSP securities facility—for their liquidity management requirements.

Bangko Sentral ng Pilipinas Approves Second-Phase Amendments on Foreign Currency Deposit System Regulations

In December, the BSP approved the second phase of amendments to regulations on the foreign currency deposit system. In the amendments, the BSP will allow Islamic banks and digital banks to engage in foreign exchange transactions and streamline the related licensing requirements for banks applying for foreign currency deposit unit (FCDU) authority. Authorized banks will only have to notify the BSP of their intention to engage in FCDU operations as compared to previous rules that prior approval from the BSP was required before they can engage in such transactions. The amendments also rationalized the prescriptive requirements for certain FCDU transactions such as those involving foreign currency derivatives and securities.

Singapore

Singapore and the People's Republic of China Strengthen Financial Cooperation

On 29 December, Monetary Authority of Singapore (MAS) announced several initiatives to promote financial cooperation between Singapore and the People's Republic of China. To allow broader access for Singaporean investors to the bond market of the People's Republic of China, Singapore Exchange and China Foreign Exchange Trade System are exploring ways to connect the two exchanges' bond trading platforms. To develop green finance, MAS and the People's Bank of China committed to look into public–private partnership in coming up with clear definitions of green activities and promoting green financial technology. These initiatives aim to foster inclusive financial growth for both economies.

Monetary Authority of Singapore and Bank Indonesia Deepen Bilateral Collaboration

On 21 January, MAS and Bank Indonesia committed to strengthening their cooperation through a memorandum of understanding. The document highlighted the commitment of the two economies to cooperate with each other when it comes to central bank functions. Among other functions, MAS and Bank Indonesia agreed to collaborate on fostering payment innovation and fighting money laundering and the financing of terrorism. The two central banks also committed to partnering in developing digital innovations in finance.

Thailand

Bank of Thailand Adjusts Bond Issuance to Accommodate Government Borrowing and Promote the Thai Overnight Repurchase Rate

On 4 January, the Bank of Thailand (BOT) announced its bond issuance program for 2022. The new issuance schedule considered the government's borrowing requirements to fund COVID-19 relief measures as well as the need to promote the development of the Thai Overnight Repurchase Rate (THOR). To accommodate the Public Debt Management Office's plan to increase issuance of 3- to 5-year bonds, the BOT will reduce the issuance frequency and reopening of its 2-year fixed rate bonds in 2022. In addition, the BOT will not issue new 6-month bills or 3-year fixed rate bonds in 2022, as the Public Debt Management Office will auction bonds with those tenors. To further develop the use of THOR as a new reference rate, the BOT will increase the auction size of 6-month and 1-year THOR-linked floating-rate bonds. The BOT will also start auctioning new 2-year THOR-linked floating-rate bonds in June.

Viet Nam

State Bank of Viet Nam Regulates Corporate Bond Transactions

In November, the State Bank of Viet Nam issued Circular No. 16/2021/TT-NHNN on regulating the purchase and sale of corporate bonds by credit institutions and foreign bank branches. Corporate bonds must satisfy the following conditions before a transaction can proceed: (i) issued in accordance with the law, (ii) denominated in Vietnamese dong; and (iii) under the legal ownership of the seller and not yet mature for principal and interest payment. The seller must also confirm that corporate bonds are not in dispute; are permitted for transactions under law; and are not in a state of being traded with a term, discounted, or rediscounted. Corporate bond issuance in the following cases is prohibited: (i) to restructure debts of the bond-issuing enterprise, (ii) to contribute capital or purchase shares at another enterprise, and (iii) to raise working capital. A credit institution may purchase corporate bonds only when its nonperforming loan ratio is under 3%.[7]

7 LuatVietnam. 2021. Circular 16/2021/TT-NHNN Prescribing the Purchase and Sale of Corporate Bonds by Credit Institutions and Foreign Bank Branches. September. https://english.luatvietnam.vn/circular-no-16-2021-tt-nhnn-dated-november-10-2021-of-the-state-bank-of-vietnam-prescribing-the-purchase-and-sale-of-corporate-bonds-by-credit-insti-212774-Doc1.html.

AsianBondsOnline Annual Bond Market Liquidity Survey

Introduction

AsianBondsOnline conducts a bond market liquidity survey every year to better understand the evolving local currency (LCY) bond market environment in emerging East Asian economies and to provide a deeper assessment of the bond market's overall structure.[8] The survey's goal is to identify factors limiting the proper functioning of the region's bond markets in terms of liquidity. This assessment will help policy makers and regulators identify areas that help further deepen their respective bond markets.

The 2021 *AsianBondsOnline* bond market liquidity survey was conducted through email, due to the ongoing coronavirus disease (COVID-19) pandemic, and involved various bond market participants including financial institutions, financial market brokers, research houses, fund managers, rating agencies, and bond pricing agencies.

The survey contains a quantitative section and a qualitative section for both LCY government and corporate bonds. While the quantitative sections for each bond market segment contain metrics such as bid–ask spreads and typical transaction sizes, the qualitative sections gather the views of survey respondents regarding the degree of bond market development along identified structural factors.

In the most recent survey, 50% of respondents indicated an annual increase in bond market liquidity in 2021, compared to 53% of respondents in 2020, while 36% of participants indicated a decline in liquidity in 2021, compared to 38% in 2020. Meanwhile, 14% of respondents in 2021 noted that liquidity was unchanged, compared to 9% in 2020. Within the region, the Republic of Korea, Malaysia, and the Philippines had the highest levels of respondents indicating that liquidity had declined in 2021 (**Figure 23**).

Figure 23: Liquidity Conditions by Economy in Emerging East Asia, 2020 versus 2021

HKG = Hong Kong, China; INO = Indonesia; KOR = Republic of Korea; MAL = Malaysia; PHI = Philippines; PRC = People's Republic of China; SIN = Singapore; THA = Thailand; VIE = Viet Nam.
Note: Figures refer to the share of survey respondents indicating either "no change," "decreased," or "increased."
Source: *AsianBondsOnline* 2021 Local Currency Bond Market Liquidity Survey.

Market sentiment was the most reported factor affecting bond market liquidity in 2021 (**Figure 24**). Over 70% of survey participants said that market sentiment was a factor driving bond market liquidity in 2021, a similar finding to that of the previous year's survey. Domestic bond yield movements, domestic monetary policy, and the pandemic also received relatively high shares of votes as factors affecting bond market liquidity. Consistent with current market conditions—marked by modest regional inflation and persistently high United States (US) inflation—market participants identified global inflationary pressure as a more significant factor than domestic inflation in 2021. Meanwhile, US monetary policy's relative impact on bond market liquidity rose from a ranking of seventh in 2020 to fifth in 2021.

---

[8] In the context of the *AsianBondsOnline* 2021 Annual Bond Market Liquidity Survey, emerging East Asia comprises the People's Republic of China; Hong Kong, China; Indonesia; the Republic of Korea; Malaysia; the Philippines; Singapore; Thailand; and Viet Nam.

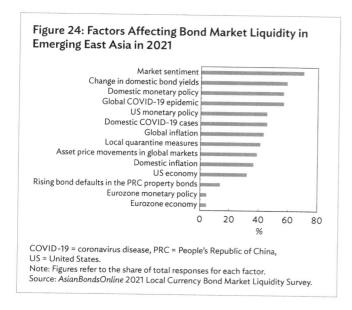

Figure 24: Factors Affecting Bond Market Liquidity in Emerging East Asia in 2021

COVID-19 = coronavirus disease, PRC = People's Republic of China, US = United States.
Note: Figures refer to the share of total responses for each factor.
Source: *AsianBondsOnline* 2021 Local Currency Bond Market Liquidity Survey.

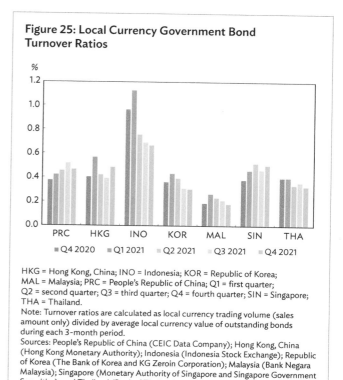

Figure 25: Local Currency Government Bond Turnover Ratios

HKG = Hong Kong, China; INO = Indonesia; KOR = Republic of Korea; MAL = Malaysia; PRC = People's Republic of China; Q1 = first quarter; Q2 = second quarter; Q3 = third quarter; Q4 = fourth quarter; SIN = Singapore; THA = Thailand.
Note: Turnover ratios are calculated as local currency trading volume (sales amount only) divided by average local currency value of outstanding bonds during each 3-month period.
Sources: People's Republic of China (CEIC Data Company); Hong Kong, China (Hong Kong Monetary Authority); Indonesia (Indonesia Stock Exchange); Republic of Korea (The Bank of Korea and KG Zeroin Corporation); Malaysia (Bank Negara Malaysia); Singapore (Monetary Authority of Singapore and Singapore Government Securities); and Thailand (Bank of Thailand and Thai Bond Market Association).

Government Bonds

Liquidity

Trends in turnover ratios for government bonds varied across markets in 2021. Quarterly government bond turnover ratios declined from the previous year in Indonesia, the Republic of Korea, and Malaysia, while they rose in the People's Republic of China (PRC) and Singapore (**Figure 25**).

In the case of Indonesia, while survey participants perceived that liquidity conditions had improved in 2021, the turnover ratio in the LCY bond market fell as the amount of available bonds for trading was curtailed by increases in the holdings of central bank and domestic long-term investors who tend to pursue a buy-and-hold strategy. In nominal terms, however, annual trading volume increased between 2020 and 2021. Overall liquidity conditions also remained ample due to Bank Indonesia's accommodative monetary policy stance. In the Republic of Korea, liquidity was affected by monetary policy adjustments as the Bank of Korea tightened monetary policy in August, November, and (more recently) in January 2022. In Malaysia, investor sentiment soured due to political concerns.

On the other hand, the turnover ratios in the PRC and Singapore trended upward in 2021. For the PRC, the turnover ratio's steady rise in the first 3 quarters of the year was buoyed by increased interest from foreign investors. The ratio dipped in the fourth quarter (Q4) of 2021 due to concerns of an economic slowdown and negative investor sentiment over rising bond defaults in the property sector. This led the People's Bank of China to lower its reserve requirement ratio in December for a second time in 2021 following an earlier rate cut in July. In addition, the People's Bank of China reduced by 10 basis points (bps) its 1-year medium-term lending facility rate in January 2022. Monetary Authority of Singapore also engaged in tightening measures in October and again in January 2022.

Survey results indicated a marginal uptick in the region's average bid–ask spread for government bonds in 2021 to 3.1 bps, compared with 2.8 bps in the prior year (**Figure 26**). Five out of nine regional markets had wider bid–ask spreads for government bonds in 2021 versus 2020. However, the increases were marginal (less than 1 bp) in the Republic of Korea, Singapore, and Thailand. On the other hand, Malaysia and the Philippines witnessed relatively larger increases in their respective spreads of 1.3 bps and 2.2 bps. Meanwhile, quoted bid–ask spreads for the PRC; Hong Kong, China; Indonesia; and Viet Nam were lower in 2021 than in 2020. In Hong Kong, China; Indonesia; and Viet Nam;

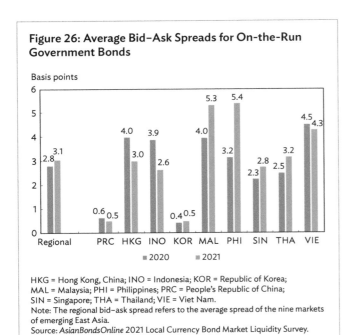

Figure 26: Average Bid–Ask Spreads for On-the-Run Government Bonds

Basis points

HKG = Hong Kong, China; INO = Indonesia; KOR = Republic of Korea;
MAL = Malaysia; PHI = Philippines; PRC = People's Republic of China;
SIN = Singapore; THA = Thailand; VIE = Viet Nam.
Note: The regional bid–ask spread refers to the average spread of the nine markets of emerging East Asia.
Source: *AsianBondsOnline* 2021 Local Currency Bond Market Liquidity Survey.

Figure 27: Average Bid–Ask Spreads for Off-the-Run Government Bonds

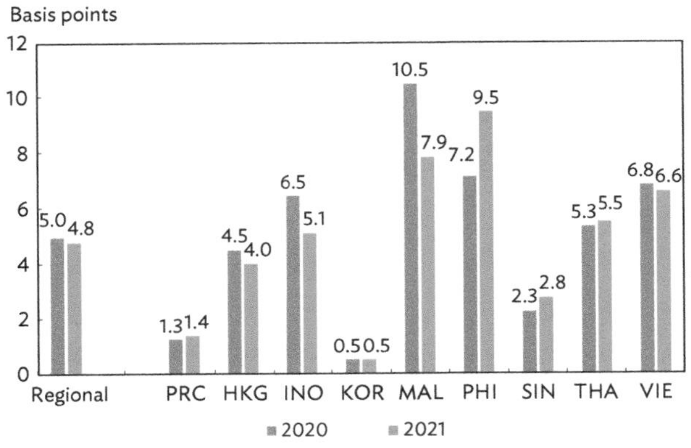

Basis points

HKG = Hong Kong, China; INO = Indonesia; KOR = Republic of Korea;
MAL = Malaysia; PHI = Philippines; PRC = People's Republic of China;
SIN = Singapore; THA = Thailand; VIE = Viet Nam.
Note: The regional bid–ask spread refers to the average spread of the nine markets of emerging East Asia.
Source: *AsianBondsOnline* 2021 Local Currency Bond Market Liquidity Survey.

narrowing bid–ask spreads resulted from abundant liquidity due to a relatively accommodative monetary policy environment. In the PRC, the decline also tracked increased foreign investor demand following the PRC's inclusion in global bond indices and given the continued pace of its economic recovery.

The regional average bid–ask spread for off-the run government bonds improved slightly to 4.8 bps in the 2021 survey from 5.0 bps in the 2020 survey (**Figure 27**). The lowest bid–ask spreads remained those of the Republic of Korea (0.5 bps) and the PRC (1.4 bps), while the Philippines (9.5 bps) and Malaysia (7.9 bps) had the widest spreads. Compared with 2020, survey participants in 2021 quoted lower spreads for off-the-run bonds in Hong Kong, China; Indonesia; Malaysia; and Viet Nam. In the PRC, the Philippines, Singapore, and Thailand, off-the-run bid–ask spreads rose, while the spread remained unchanged in the Republic of Korea.

The region's average single-trade transaction size for on-the-run government bonds climbed to USD10.6 billion in 2021 from USD8.1 billion in 2020 (**Figure 28**). The rise was largely fueled by the increased transaction size of a single trade in Hong Kong, China in 2021, which itself was driven by a high degree of liquidity in the banking system. The increased demand also led the Hong Kong Monetary Authority to raise its issuance

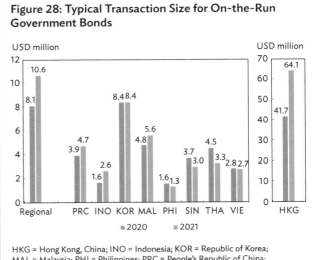

Figure 28: Typical Transaction Size for On-the-Run Government Bonds

USD million

HKG = Hong Kong, China; INO = Indonesia; KOR = Republic of Korea;
MAL = Malaysia; PHI = Philippines; PRC = People's Republic of China;
SIN = Singapore; THA = Thailand; USD = United States dollar; VIE = Viet Nam.
Note: The regional bid–ask spread refers to the average spread of the nine markets of emerging East Asia.
Source: *AsianBondsOnline* 2021 Local Currency Bond Market Liquidity Survey.

volume of Exchange Fund Bills between September and December. To a lesser extent, growth in the average government bond transaction size in the PRC (from USD3.9 million in 2020 to USD4.7 million in 2021) and Indonesia (from USD1.6 million to USD2.6 million) also contributed to the higher regional average for 2021. Results from the 2021 survey showed that the average transaction size was the largest in Hong Kong, China (USD64.1 million) and the lowest in Indonesia (USD2.6 million) and the Philippines (USD1.3 million).

Market Development

The survey also includes the qualitative assessments of participants on a set of structural factors that describe developments in the region's government bond markets. There are eight structural factors that participants were asked to rate on a scale from 1 to 4. A higher rating indicates that the structural factor is either widely available or developed in that market, while a lower rating indicates its nonavailability or underdevelopment.

The 2021 qualitative survey results for emerging East Asian government bond markets showed improvement from the previous year on structural factors on average, with all factors having a regional average score above 3.0 except for hedging mechanisms (**Figure 29**).

Transparency received the highest average score in 2021 of 3.6, increasing from 3.4 in 2020. With most markets

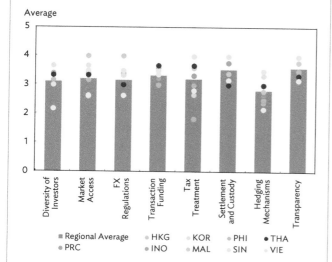

Figure 29: Local Currency Government Bond Market Structural Issues in Emerging East Asia

HKG = Hong Kong, China; FX = foreign exchange; INO = Indonesia; KOR = Republic of Korea; MAL = Malaysia; PHI = Philippines; PRC = People's Republic of China; SIN = Singapore; THA = Thailand; VIE = Viet Nam.
Note: Emerging East Asia comprises the People's Republic of China; Hong Kong, China; Indonesia; the Republic of Korea; Malaysia; the Philippines; Singapore; Thailand; and Viet Nam.
Source: *AsianBondsOnline* 2021 Local Currency Bond Market Liquidity Survey.

adapting technology, such as the use of online platforms, bond information is becoming more available and easily accessible. Hong Kong, China; the Republic of Korea; and Singapore—which are known to have well-developed bond markets—had scores of 4.0 each.

Settlement and custody had an average score of 3.5 in 2021. While this was the second-highest rating among all structural factors, the score inched down from 3.7 in 2020. Nonetheless, the high rating reflects that the systems governing the region's bond markets are capable of facilitating the efficient settlement of bond trade transactions. All regional markets had a score of 3.0 or above, with the markets of Hong Kong, China; the Republic of Korea; and Singapore each scoring 4.0. In 2021, Hong Kong, China launched a delivery-versus-payment link for cross-currency securities transactions between the Hong Kong Dollar Clearing House Automated Transfer System and the Bank of Japan Financial Network System.

Transaction Funding scored an average of 3.3 in 2021, unchanged from the previous year, indicating that active and developed money and repurchase markets are present in individual emerging East Asian markets. The markets with the lowest scores in the region in 2021 were Hong Kong, China; Malaysia; and the Philippines at 3.0 each.

Tax Treatment obtained a regional average score of 3.2 in 2021. Markets like Hong Kong, China and Singapore with tax exemption on interest income from government bond investments were rated 4.0 by survey respondents, while the Philippines, which levies a 20% tax on interest income, had the region's lowest rating at 1.8. In Indonesia, the withholding tax on bond investments for both domestic and foreign investors was reduced in 2021 to 10% from 15% to encourage greater participation and enhance liquidity.

Market Access and Foreign Exchange Regulations were both given an average score of 3.2 in 2021, as regional bond markets continued to improve investor access to bonds. The Hong Kong Monetary Authority and the People's Bank of China announced the opening of the southbound leg of the Bond Connect scheme, which will allow residents in the PRC to buy bonds in Hong Kong, China. On foreign exchange regulations, the PRC and the Philippines both undertook liberalization measures in 2021 to facilitate foreign exchange transactions.[9]

Diversity of Investors had an average score of 3.1, the second-lowest rating among all structural factors, albeit an improvement compared to 2020's score of 2.9. All regional markets had a score of 3.0 or above except for Viet Nam, which had a score of 2.2, reflecting the small size of its bond market that is dominated by investors from the banking and insurance sectors.

Hedging Mechanisms remained the lowest-rated structural factor among survey participants. It scored an average of 2.8 in 2021, up slightly from 2.7 in 2020. Most markets had a score below 3.0. The Republic of Korea (3.3) and Singapore (3.5) had the highest scores in the region, owing to their developed markets. Though it posted the region's lowest score (2.2), Viet Nam added a hedging instrument in 2021 with the launch of a 10-year government bond future to provide another risk prevention tool for long-term government bonds.

Corporate Bond Markets

Liquidity

Corporate bond markets in emerging East Asia continued to be less liquid than government bond markets, as most corporate bonds in the region are held to maturity. For 2021, the region's corporate bond markets showed improved liquidity, with more survey participants noting an active secondary market in 2021 (85%) compared to 2020 (67%) (**Figure 30**). In the Philippines and Viet Nam, participants noted corporate bond trading activity in 2021 following inactivity in 2020.

The improvement in liquidity in 2021 was supported by narrower bid–ask spreads for most markets in the region. The regional average declined to 16.3 bps from 22.2 bps in 2020 (**Figure 31**). Six markets posted lower bid–ask spreads in 2021, including the PRC; Hong Kong, China; Indonesia; Malaysia; Singapore; and Viet Nam. Viet Nam registered the largest decline in its average bid–ask spread, from 85.0 bps in 2020 to 60.8 bps in 2021, as market participants noted increased liquidity in the corporate bond market in 2021 compared to a lack of trading activity in 2020. Indonesia posted the second-largest decline,

Figure 30: Is There an Active Secondary Bond Market?

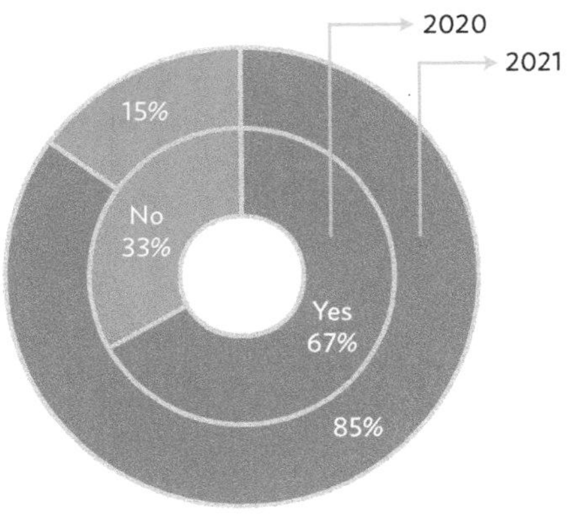

Note: Percentages refer to the share of survey respondents answering either "yes" or "no."
Source: *AsianBondsOnline* 2021 Local Currency Bond Market Liquidity Survey.

Figure 31: Average Bid–Ask Spreads for Corporate Bonds

HKG = Hong Kong, China; INO = Indonesia; KOR = Republic of Korea; MAL = Malaysia; PHI = Philippines; PRC = People's Republic of China; SIN = Singapore; THA = Thailand; VIE = Viet Nam.
Note: The regional bid–ask spread refers to the average spread of the nine markets of emerging East Asia.
Source: *AsianBondsOnline* 2021 Local Currency Bond Market Liquidity Survey.

from 15.9 bps in 2020 to 7.0 bps in 2021, due to improved overall liquidity conditions in the market. Meanwhile, the Philippines and Thailand registered an increase in their bid–ask spreads but with only an average increment of 1.9 bps in each market. The Republic of Korea's average bid–ask spread barely changed between 2020 and 2021, with a marginal increase of less than 1 basis point. Viet Nam and the Philippines continued to post the region's widest corporate bid–ask spreads at 60.8 bps and

---

[9] For the PRC, see https://asia.nikkei.com/Spotlight/Caixin/China-tries-more-flexibility-for-multinational-currency-exchange. For the Philippines, see https://www.bsp.gov.ph/SitePages/MediaAndResearch/MediaDisp.aspx?ItemId=5892.

40.0 bps, respectively, as their corporate bond markets remained relatively underdeveloped with most investors holding their bonds until maturity.

The region's average corporate bond market transaction size increased to USD3.4 million from USD2.7 million in 2020, with six out of nine markets posting larger average transaction sizes in the 2021 survey compared with a year earlier (**Figure 32**). Viet Nam's corporate bond market registered the largest increase in average transaction size, rising from USD2.2 million to USD4.9 million. The increase and the relatively large average transaction size in Viet Nam can be traced to the surge in corporate bond issuance in 2021 and may also be due to the few very large investors participating in trading. The PRC registered the second-largest increase from USD3.1 million in 2020 to USD4.7 million in 2021, which can also be attributed to increased corporate bond issuances in 2021 despite a rising number of bond defaults, as the domestic economy rebounded. The three markets with the smallest average transaction sizes include Thailand (USD0.8 million), Indonesia (USD0.6 million), and the Philippines (USD0.4 million). The corporate bond markets of Hong Kong, China and the Republic of Korea continued to have the largest average transaction sizes at USD8.3 million and USD6.6 million, respectively.

Between Q4 2020 and Q4 2021, changes in turnover ratios for the corporate bond markets in the region

for which data are available were mixed (**Figure 33**). Corporate turnover ratios in the PRC rose the most, from 0.16 in Q4 2020 to 0.33 in Q4 2021, as both trading volume and average bonds outstanding posted annual increases, with trading volume doubling in size during the year. For the Republic of Korea and Malaysia, corporate turnover ratios showed increases in the first half of 2021, but then slightly declined in the second half of the year. For Thailand, the corporate turnover ratio remained relatively steady during the review period. Meanwhile, the corporate turnover ratio fell in Indonesia from 0.26 in Q4 2020 to 0.19 in Q4 2021, as trading volume fell at a faster pace than average bonds outstanding. The turnover ratio in Hong Kong, China fell from 0.15 to 0.08 during the review period due to a decline in trading volume.

Market Development

Compared to the 2020 liquidity survey, the development of the region's corporate bond market was generally similar in 2021. The corporate bond market of emerging East Asia continued to be well-developed when it comes to settlement and custody, transaction funding, foreign exchange regulations, market access, and transparency (**Figure 34**). Each of these categories had an average

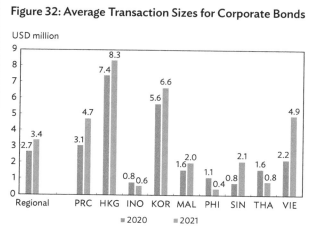

Figure 32: Average Transaction Sizes for Corporate Bonds

HKG = Hong Kong, China; INO = Indonesia; KOR = Republic of Korea; MAL = Malaysia; PHI = Philippines; PRC = People's Republic of China; SIN = Singapore; THA = Thailand; USD = United States dollar; VIE = Viet Nam.
Note: The regional bid–ask spread refers to the average spread of the nine markets of emerging East Asia.
Source: *AsianBondsOnline* 2021 Local Currency Bond Market Liquidity Survey.

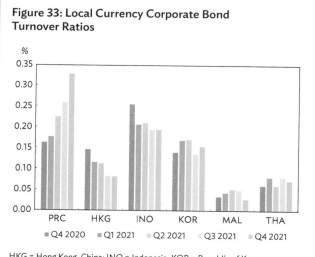

Figure 33: Local Currency Corporate Bond Turnover Ratios

HKG = Hong Kong, China; INO = Indonesia; KOR = Republic of Korea; MAL = Malaysia; PRC = People's Republic of China; Q1 = first quarter; Q2 = second quarter; Q3 = third quarter; Q4 = fourth quarter; THA = Thailand.
Note: Turnover ratios are calculated as local currency trading volume (sales amount only) divided by average local currency value of outstanding bonds during each 3-month period.
Sources: People's Republic of China (CEIC Data Company); Hong Kong, China (Hong Kong Monetary Authority); Indonesia (Indonesia Stock Exchange); Republic of Korea (The Bank of Korea and KG Zeroin Corporation); Malaysia (Bank Negara Malaysia); Singapore (Monetary Authority of Singapore and Singapore Government Securities); and Thailand (Bank of Thailand and Thai Bond Market Association).

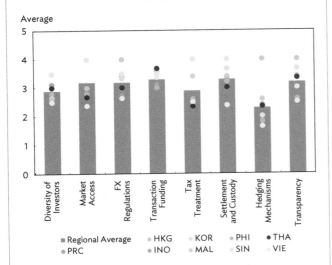

Figure 34: Local Currency Corporate Bond Market Structural Issues in Emerging East Asia

Average

HKG = Hong Kong, China; FX = foreign exchange; INO = Indonesia; KOR = Republic of Korea; MAL = Malaysia; PHI = Philippines; PRC = People's Republic of China; SIN = Singapore; THA = Thailand; VIE = Viet Nam.
Note: Emerging East Asia comprises the People's Republic of China; Hong Kong, China; Indonesia; the Republic of Korea; Malaysia; the Philippines; Singapore; Thailand; and Viet Nam.
Source: AsianBondsOnline 2021 Local Currency Bond Market Liquidity Survey.

score of 3.0 or above in the 2021 survey. On the other hand, survey participants deemed that improvements were needed in terms of diversity of the investor profile, tax treatment, and hedging mechanisms.

Emerging East Asia's corporate bond market received an average score of 3.3 in settlement and custody, with Viet Nam scoring the lowest among all markets. Transaction funding also scored a regional average of 3.3. Foreign exchange regulations, market access, and transparency in regional corporate bond markets scored relatively high at 3.2 each.

Two areas that need improvement in the corporate bond market of emerging East Asia are investor profile diversity and taxation, with both categories receiving a score of 2.9. (Except for Hong Kong, China, all markets in the region levy tax on interest income on corporate bonds.)

The structural factor with the lowest score for the region's corporate bond market in 2021 was hedging mechanisms, which logged an average score of 2.3. Almost all markets in the region lack the tools needed by investors to effectively manage risk.

Market Summaries

People's Republic of China

Local currency (LCY) bonds outstanding in the People's Republic of China (PRC) grew 3.9% quarter-on-quarter (q-o-q) in the fourth quarter (Q4) of 2021 to reach CNY115.1 trillion (USD18.1 trillion). The q-o-q growth in bonds outstanding was roughly stable as the government continued borrowing to help arrest a slowdown in the PRC's economy. Local governments saw an increase in the growth rate of their bonds outstanding to 5.8% q-o-q in Q4 2021 from 4.9% q-o-q in the previous quarter. The accelerated pace of expansion was driven by efforts to complete their full-year bond quotas. The PRC's LCY bonds outstanding rose 13.6% year-on-year (y-o-y) in Q4 2021, up from 12.8% y-o-y in the third quarter of 2021.

Table 1: Size and Composition of the Local Currency Bond Market in the People's Republic of China

| | Outstanding Amount (billion) | | | | | | Growth Rates (%) | | | |
| | Q4 2020 | | Q3 2021 | | Q4 2021 | | Q4 2020 | | Q4 2021 | |
	CNY	USD	CNY	USD	CNY	USD	q-o-q	y-o-y	q-o-q	y-o-y
Total	101,413	15,537	110,784	17,190	115,154	18,117	3.3	20.5	3.9	13.6
Government	65,130	9,978	71,171	11,043	74,373	11,701	3.8	20.6	4.5	14.2
Treasury Bonds	20,933	3,207	22,370	3,471	23,420	3,685	8.3	25.4	4.7	11.9
Central Bank Bonds	15	2	15	2	15	2	0.0	(31.8)	0.0	0.0
Policy Bank Bonds	18,040	2,764	19,253	2,987	19,681	3,096	3.2	14.9	2.2	9.1
Local Government Bonds	26,142	4,005	29,533	4,583	31,257	4,918	0.9	21.2	5.8	19.6
Corporate	36,283	5,559	39,613	6,146	40,781	6,416	2.4	20.1	2.9	12.4

( ) = negative, – = not applicable, CNY = Chinese yuan, LCY = local currency, q-o-q = quarter-on-quarter, Q3 = third quarter, Q4 = fourth quarter, USD = United States dollar, y-o-y = year-on-year.
Notes:
1. Treasury bonds include savings bonds and local government bonds.
2. Bloomberg LP end-of-period LCY–USD rate is used.
3. Growth rates are calculated from an LCY base and do not include currency effects.
Sources: CEIC and Bloomberg LP.

Total LCY corporate bond issuance in the PRC grew 3.9% q-o-q to CNY5.2 trillion in 2021. On a y-o-y basis, LCY corporate bond issuance grew 13.9%. A number of financial institutions issued long-term bonds and perpetual bonds as part of their capital-raising efforts in Q4 2021.

Table 2: Notable Local Currency Corporate Bond Issuances in the Fourth Quarter of 2021

Corporate Issuers	Coupon Rate (%)	Issued Amount (CNY billion)
China State Railway Group Co[a]		
5-year bond	3.11	10
10-year bond	3.47	15
10-year bond	3.39	10
10-year bond	3.51	10
10-year bond	3.39	10
20-year bond	3.74	10
30-year bond	3.73	10
30-year bond	3.75	10
30-year bond	3.77	10
30-year bond	3.82	5
Industrial Bank[a]		
5-year bond	0.20	50
10-year bond	3.62	40
10-year bond	3.83	30

Corporate Issuers	Coupon Rate (%)	Issued Amount (CNY billion)
Industrial and Commercial Bank of China		
5-year bond	3.74	10
10-year bond	3.48	50
Perpetual bond	3.65	30
Bank of China		
5-year bond	3.80	10
10-year bond	3.60	40
Perpetual bond	3.64	20
China Construction Bank[a]		
10-year bond	3.60	35
10-year bond	3.48	12
15-year bond	3.80	10
15-year bond	3.74	8

CNY = Chinese yuan.
[a] Multiple issuance of the same tenor indicates issuance on different dates.
Source: Bloomberg LP.

At the end of December, the aggregate amount of corporate bonds outstanding of the PRC's top 30 issuers grew to CNY11.6 trillion, which comprised 28.5% of the total corporate bond market. China Railway remained the dominant issuer by a wide margin with a CNY3,000.5 billion of bonds outstanding. The second-largest issuer, Industrial and Commercial Bank of China, had outstanding bonds of CNY761.1 billion.

Table 3: Top 30 Issuers of Local Currency Corporate Bonds in the People's Republic of China

	Issuers	Outstanding Amount		State-Owned	Listed Company	Type of Industry
		LCY Bonds (CNY billion)	LCY Bonds (USD billion)			
1.	China Railway	3,000.5	472.1	Yes	No	Transportation
2.	Industrial and Commercial Bank of China	761.1	119.7	Yes	Yes	Banking
3.	Bank of China	738.1	116.1	Yes	Yes	Banking
4.	Agricultural Bank of China	690.0	108.6	Yes	Yes	Banking
5.	Bank of Communications	519.9	81.8	Yes	Yes	Banking
6.	China Construction Bank	493.1	77.6	Yes	No	Asset Management
7.	Shanghai Pudong Development Bank	492.2	77.4	Yes	Yes	Banking
8.	Central Huijin Investment	407.0	64.0	No	Yes	Banking
9.	State Grid Corporation of China	368.5	58.0	No	Yes	Banking
10.	Industrial Bank	331.2	52.1	No	Yes	Banking
11.	China Citic Bank	315.0	49.6	No	Yes	Banking
12.	China Minsheng Bank	270.0	42.5	Yes	No	Energy
13.	China National Petroleum	269.9	42.5	No	Yes	Banking
14.	State Power Investment	258.8	40.7	Yes	No	Power
15.	China Merchants Bank	252.2	39.7	Yes	Yes	Banking
16.	Huaxia Bank	220.0	34.6	No	Yes	Banking
17.	China Everbright Bank	215.9	34.0	No	Yes	Banking
18.	Postal Savings Bank of China	190.0	29.9	Yes	Yes	Coal
19.	Ping An Bank	180.0	28.3	No	Yes	Banking
20.	China Southern Power Grid	178.9	28.1	No	Yes	Banking
21.	Huatai Securities	176.5	27.8	No	No	Brokerage
22.	CITIC Securities	176.3	27.7	Yes	No	Public Utilities
23.	Tianjin Infrastructure Investment Group	154.2	24.3	Yes	Yes	Brokerage
24.	GF Securities	153.9	24.2	No	Yes	Brokerage
25.	Shaanxi Coal and Chemical Industry Group	152.0	23.9	No	Yes	Brokerage
26.	Shenwan Hongyuan Securities	141.5	22.3	Yes	No	Brokerage
27.	Guotai Junan Securities Co Ltd	140.7	22.1	No	Yes	Brokerage
28.	China Merchants Securities	140.6	22.1	Yes	Yes	Brokerage
29.	Bank of Beijing	127.9	20.1	No	Yes	Banking
30.	Haitong Securities	122.3	19.2	Yes	Yes	Brokerage
	Total Top 30 LCY Corporate Issuers	11,638.2	1,831.0			
	Total LCY Corporate Bonds	40,781.4	6,416.1			
	Top 30 as % of Total LCY Corporate Bonds	28.5%	28.5%			

CNY = Chinese yuan, LCY = local currency, USD = United States dollar.
Notes:
1. Data as of 31 December 2021.
2. State-owned firms are defined as those in which the government has more than a 50% ownership stake.
Source: *AsianBondsOnline* calculations based on Bloomberg LP data.

Hong Kong, China

The local currency (LCY) bond market in Hong Kong, China expanded to a size of HKD2,525.0 billion (USD323.9 billion) at the end of the fourth quarter (Q4) of 2021. Overall growth accelerated to 4.0% quarter-on-quarter (q-o-q) in Q4 2021 from 0.1% q-o-q in the previous quarter, buoyed by more rapid expansion in the government bond segment and a rebound in the corporate bond segment. The Hong Kong Monetary Authority increased issuance of Exchange Fund Bills in Q4 2021 to meet strong market demand amid ample liquidity in the banking system.

Table 1: Size and Composition of the Local Currency Bond Market in Hong Kong, China

| | Outstanding Amount (billion) | | | | | | Growth Rate (%) | | | |
| | Q4 2020 | | Q3 2021 | | Q4 2021 | | Q4 2020 | | Q4 2021 | |
	HKD	USD	HKD	USD	HKD	USD	q-o-q	y-o-y	q-o-q	y-o-y
Total	2,405	310	2,429	312	2,525	324	5.1	6.1	4.0	5.0
Government	1,185	153	1,252	161	1,317	169	2.3	0.2	5.2	11.2
Exchange Fund Bills	1,043	135	1,064	137	1,125	144	0.1	(1.2)	5.7	7.9
Exchange Fund Notes	25	3	24	3	23	3	(3.1)	(6.0)	(3.3)	(6.4)
HKSAR Bonds	117	15	164	21	168	22	30.1	16.3	2.7	44.4
Corporate	1,220	157	1,176	151	1,208	155	7.9	12.6	2.7	(1.0)

( ) = negative, HKD = Hong Kong dollar, HKSAR = Hong Kong Special Administrative Region, LCY = local currency, q-o-q = quarter-on-quarter, Q3 = third quarter, Q4 = fourth quarter, USD = United States dollar, y-o-y = year-on-year.
Notes:
1. Bloomberg LP end-of-period LCY–USD rates are used.
2. Growth rates are calculated from an LCY base and do not include currency effects.
Source: Hong Kong Monetary Authority.

Issuance of LCY corporate bonds rose to HKD204.9 billion in Q4 2021 from HKD196.7 billion in the third quarter of 2021. Growth rebounded to 4.2% q-o-q in Q4 2021, following a contraction of 15.8% q-o-q in the previous quarter. State-owned Hong Kong Monetary Mortgage Corporation was the top nonbank corporate issuer in Q4 2021.

Table 2: Notable Local Currency Corporate Bond Issuances in the Fourth Quarter of 2021

Corporate Issuers	Coupon Rate (%)	Issued Amount (HKD million)
Hong Kong Mortgage Corporation		
1-year bond	0.29	800
2-year bond	0.74	1,000
3-year bond	0.83	1,000
5-year bond	1.54	100
10-year bond	2.00	120
Farsail Goldman International		
5-year bond	7.00	2,418
Wheelock and Company[a]		
3-year bond	1.65	400
5-year bond	2.05	500
5-year bond	2.00	300
9.25-year bond	2.35	200
10-year bond	2.50	200
Link Holdings		
5-year bond	1.48	800
9.97-year bond	2.23	782

HKD = Hong Kong dollar.
[a] Multiple issuance of the same tenor indicates issuance on different dates.
Source: Bloomberg LP.

The outstanding bonds of the top 30 nonbank corporate issuers in Hong Kong, China amounted to HKD304.1 billion at the end of December, accounting for a 25.2% share of the LCY corporate bond market. Hong Kong Mortgage Corporation remained the top issuer, with outstanding bonds amounting to HKD72.8 billion. Over half of the top 30 list in Q4 2021 comprised finance and real estate companies.

Table 3: Top 30 Nonbank Issuers of Local Currency Corporate Bonds in Hong Kong, China

	Issuers	Outstanding Amount		State-Owned	Listed Company	Type of Industry
		LCY Bonds (HKD billion)	LCY Bonds (USD billion)			
1.	Hong Kong Mortgage Corporation	72.8	9.3	Yes	No	Finance
2.	Sun Hung Kai & Co.	20.6	2.6	No	Yes	Finance
3.	The Hong Kong and China Gas Company	18.0	2.3	No	Yes	Utilities
4.	New World Development	16.0	2.0	No	Yes	Diversified
5.	Link Holdings	13.7	1.8	No	Yes	Finance
6.	Hang Lung Properties	13.2	1.7	No	Yes	Real Estate
7.	Hongkong Land	12.4	1.6	No	No	Real Estate
8.	Henderson Land Development	12.3	1.6	No	Yes	Real Estate
9.	MTR	12.0	1.5	Yes	Yes	Transportation
10.	Swire Pacific	10.1	1.3	No	Yes	Diversified
11.	CK Asset Holdings	10.0	1.3	No	Yes	Real Estate
12.	The Wharf Holdings	9.7	1.2	No	Yes	Finance
13.	Cathay Pacific	9.0	1.1	No	Yes	Transportation
14.	Airport Authority	8.9	1.1	Yes	No	Transportation
15.	Hongkong Electric	8.5	1.1	No	No	Utilities
16.	Guotai Junan International Holdings	7.5	1.0	No	Yes	Finance
17.	CLP Power Hong Kong Financing	7.4	0.9	No	No	Finance
18.	Swire Properties	7.3	0.9	No	Yes	Diversified
19.	Hysan Development Corporation	6.1	0.8	No	Yes	Real Estate
20.	Haitong International	3.7	0.5	No	Yes	Finance
21.	Future Days	3.7	0.5	No	No	Transportation
22.	Lerthai Group	3.0	0.4	No	Yes	Real Estate
23.	Wheelock and Company	2.9	0.4	No	Yes	Real Estate
24.	Farsail Goldman International	2.4	0.3	No	No	Finance
25.	AIA Group	2.4	0.3	No	Yes	Insurance
26.	Ev Dynamics Holdings	2.4	0.3	No	Yes	Diversified
27.	Champion REIT	2.3	0.3	No	Yes	Real Estate
28.	South Shore Holdings	2.2	0.3	No	Yes	Industrial
29.	IFC Development	2.0	0.3	No	No	Finance
30.	Nan Fung	1.8	0.2	No	No	Real Estate
	Total Top 30 Nonbank LCY Corporate Issuers	**304.1**	**39.0**			
	Total LCY Corporate Bonds	**1,208.2**	**155.0**			
	Top 30 as % of Total LCY Corporate Bonds	**25.2%**	**25.2%**			

HKD = Hong Kong dollar, LCY = local currency, REIT = real estate investment trust, USD = United States dollar.
Notes:
1. Data as of 31 December 2021.
2. State-owned firms are defined as those in which the government has more than a 50% ownership stake.
Source: *AsianBondsOnline* calculations based on Bloomberg LP data.

Indonesia

The outstanding stock of local currency (LCY) bonds in Indonesia totaled IDR5,314.5 trillion (USD372.6 billion) at the end of December, expanding 4.4% quarter-on-quarter (q-o-q) and 17.7% year-on-year in the fourth quarter (Q4) of 2021. Much of the growth was driven by government bonds issued to support fiscal spending to strengthen the economic recovery.

Table 1: Size and Composition of the Local Currency Bond Market in Indonesia

| | Outstanding Amount (billion) | | | | | | Growth Rate (%) | | | |
| | Q4 2020 | | Q3 2021 | | Q4 2021 | | Q4 2020 | | Q4 2021 | |
	IDR	USD	IDR	USD	IDR	USD	q-o-q	y-o-y	q-o-q	y-o-y
Total	4,517,251	322	5,089,510	356	5,314,547	373	10.0	28.7	4.4	17.7
Government	4,091,542	291	4,667,501	326	4,884,206	342	11.6	33.6	4.6	19.4
Central Govt. Bonds	3,870,757	275	4,460,456	312	4,678,977	328	11.8	40.6	4.9	20.9
of which: sukuk	686,561	49	834,323	58	841,973	59	11.1	41.4	0.9	22.6
Central Bank Bonds	55,421	4	60,712	4	61,337	4	44.3	(45.9)	1.0	10.7
of which: sukuk	55,421	4	60,712	4	61,337	4	44.3	(22.1)	1.0	10.7
Nontradable Bonds	165,365	12	146,334	10	143,892	10	(1.4)	(20.7)	(1.7)	(13.0)
of which: sukuk	38,778	3	31,161	2	31,666	2	1.4	(11.4)	1.6	(18.3)
Corporate	425,709	30	422,008	29	430,341	30	(3.4)	(4.4)	2.0	1.1
of which: sukuk	30,341	2	36,143	3	34,813	2	(1.9)	0.7	(3.7)	14.7

( ) = negative, IDR = Indonesian rupiah, LCY = local currency, q-o-q = quarter-on-quarter, Q3 = third quarter, Q4 = fourth quarter, USD = United States dollar, y-o-y = year-on-year.
Notes:
1. Bloomberg LP end-of-period LCY–USD rates are used.
2. Growth rates are calculated from an LCY base and do not include currency effects.
Sources: Bank Indonesia; Directorate General of Budget Financing and Risk Management, Ministry of Finance; Indonesia Stock Exchange; and Bloomberg LP.

LCY corporate bond issuance reached IDR31.2 trillion in Q4 2021, contracting 4.4% q-o-q but expanding 45.1% year-on-year. Corporate bond issuance outpaced maturities during the quarter, resulting in a slight q-o-q uptick in the total LCY corporate bond stock at the end of December. Indah Kiat Pulp & Paper led all new corporate issues in Q4 2021, tapping the bond market twice (October and December) and raising a total of IDR6.8 trillion.

Table 2: Notable Local Currency Corporate Bond Issuances in the Fourth Quarter of 2021

Corporate Issuers	Coupon Rate (%)	Issued Amount (IDR billion)		Corporate Issuers	Coupon Rate (%)	Issued Amount (IDR billion)
Indah Kiat Pulp & Paper[a]				Profesional Telekomunikasi Indonesia		
370-day bond	6.75	1,500		370-day bond	3.60	1,012
370-day bond	6.00	797		3-year bond	5.30	1,593
370-day sukuk mudharabah	6.75	500		5-year bond	6.10	744
370-day sukuk mudharabah	6.00	187		Permodalan Nasional Madani		
3-year bond	9.25	1,050		370-day bond	3.75	1,000
3-year bond	8.75	877		3-year bond	5.50	1,000
3-year sukuk mudharabah	9.25	449		5-year bond	6.25	1,000
3-year sukuk mudharabah	8.75	305				
5-year bond	10.00	450				
5-year bond	9.25	338				
5-year sukuk mudharabah	10.00	51				
5-year sukuk mudharabah	9.25	247				

IDR = Indonesian rupiah.
Note: Sukuk mudharabah are Islamic bonds backed by a profit-sharing scheme from a business venture or partnership.
[a] Multiple issuance of the same tenor indicates issuance on different dates.
Source: Indonesia Stock Exchange.

The 31 largest corporate bond issuers in Indonesia had an outstanding aggregate bond stock of IDR315.8 trillion at the end of December, accounting for 73.4% of the corporate bond total. State-owned energy firm Perusahaan Listrik Negara continued to hold the top spot with outstanding bonds of IDR36.0 trillion, representing 8.4% of the corporate bond stock. State-owned firms comprised a majority of the list (18 out of 31).

Table 3: Top 31 Issuers of Local Currency Corporate Bonds in Indonesia

	Issuers	Outstanding Amount		State-Owned	Listed Company	Type of Industry
		LCY Bonds (IDR billion)	LCY Bonds (USD billion)			
1.	Perusahaan Listrik Negara	35,986	2.52	Yes	No	Energy
2.	Indonesia Eximbank	29,000	2.03	Yes	No	Banking
3.	Sarana Multi Infrastruktur	20,513	1.44	Yes	No	Finance
4.	Bank Rakyat Indonesia	20,144	1.41	Yes	Yes	Banking
5.	Sarana Multigriya Finansial	16,851	1.18	Yes	No	Finance
6.	Indah Kiat Pulp & Paper	6,747	0.47	No	Yes	Pulp and Paper
7.	Bank Mandiri	14,000	0.98	Yes	Yes	Banking
8.	Bank Tabungan Negara	15,975	1.12	Yes	Yes	Banking
9.	Permodalan Nasional Madani	9,423	0.66	Yes	No	Finance
10.	Indosat	11,779	0.83	No	Yes	Telecommunications
11.	Waskita Karya	10,577	0.74	Yes	Yes	Building Construction
12.	Astra Sedaya Finance	7,313	0.51	No	No	Finance
13.	Pegadaian	10,305	0.72	Yes	No	Finance
14.	Pupuk Indonesia	6,296	0.44	Yes	No	Chemical Manufacturing
15.	Tower Bersama Infrastructure	3,788	0.27	No	Yes	Telecommunications Infrastructure Provider
16.	Hutama Karya	6,500	0.46	Yes	No	Nonbuilding Construction
17.	Bank Pan Indonesia	13,427	0.94	No	Yes	Banking
18.	Wijaya Karya	7,500	0.53	Yes	Yes	Building Construction
19.	Semen Indonesia	7,078	0.50	Yes	Yes	Cement Manufacturing
20.	Telekomunikasi Indonesia	7,000	0.49	Yes	Yes	Telecommunications
21.	Sinar Mas Agro Resources and Technology	4,500	0.32	No	Yes	Food
22.	Federal International Finance	5,981	0.42	No	No	Finance
23.	Adira Dinamika Multi Finance	7,639	0.54	No	Yes	Finance
24.	Chandra Asri Petrochemical	4,589	0.32	No	Yes	Petrochemicals
25.	Bank CIMB Niaga	6,806	0.48	No	Yes	Banking
26.	Mandiri Tunas Finance	4,878	0.34	No	No	Finance
27.	Bank Pembangunan Daerah Jawa Barat Dan Banten	5,248	0.37	Yes	Yes	Banking
28.	Adhi Karya	4,316	0.30	Yes	Yes	Building Construction
29.	Medco-Energi Internasional	3,690	0.26	No	Yes	Petrochemicals
30.	Kereta Api Indonesia	4,000	0.28	Yes	No	Transportation
31.	OKI Pulp & Paper Mills	4,000	0.28	No	No	Pulp and Paper Manufacturing
	Total Top 30 LCY Corporate Issuers	**315,846**	**22.14**			
	Total LCY Corporate Bonds	**430,341**	**30.17**			
	Top 30 as % of Total LCY Corporate Bonds	**73.4%**	**73.4%**			

IDR = Indonesian rupiah, LCY = local currency, USD = United States dollar.
Notes:
1. Data as of 31 December 2021.
2. State-owned firms are defined as those in which the government has more than a 50% ownership stake.
Source: *AsianBondsOnline* calculations based on Indonesia Stock Exchange data.

Republic of Korea

The Republic of Korea's local currency (LCY) bond market grew 1.5% quarter-on-quarter (q-o-q) to KRW2,841.9 trillion (USD2,388.4 billion) at the end of December, largely driven by growth in the corporate bond segment. Total LCY corporate bonds outstanding rose 2.4% q-o-q to KRW1,659.3 trillion as corporate bond issuance surged during the quarter. Meanwhile, government bonds outstanding posted minimal growth of 0.2% q-o-q to KRW1,182.6 trillion as the rise in the stock of central government bonds was offset by the decline in central bank bonds. On a year-on-year basis, the Republic of Korea's LCY bonds outstanding expanded 7.9%.

Table 1: Size and Composition of the Local Currency Bond Market in the Republic of Korea

| | Outstanding Amount (billion) | | | | | | Growth Rate (%) | | | |
| | Q4 2020 | | Q3 2021 | | Q4 2021 | | Q4 2020 | | Q4 2021 | |
	KRW	USD	KRW	USD	KRW	USD	q-o-q	y-o-y	q-o-q	y-o-y
Total	2,633,219	2,424	2,799,920	2,365	2,841,873	2,388	1.2	9.4	1.5	7.9
Government	1,078,982	993	1,179,746	996	1,182,573	994	0.9	13.3	0.2	9.6
Central Government Bonds	726,766	669	831,745	702	843,660	709	2.7	18.8	1.4	16.1
Central Bank Bonds	159,260	147	151,050	128	140,320	118	(4.5)	(2.9)	(7.1)	(11.9)
Others	192,956	178	196,951	166	198,592	167	(0.9)	9.4	0.8	2.9
Corporate	1,554,237	1,430	1,620,174	1,368	1,659,300	1,395	1.4	6.8	2.4	6.8

( ) = negative, KRW = Korean won, LCY = local currency, q-o-q = quarter-on-quarter, Q3 = third quarter, Q4 = fourth quarter, USD = United States dollar, y-o-y = year-on-year.
Notes:
1. Bloomberg LP end-of-period LCY–USD rates are used.
2. Growth rates are calculated from an LCY base and do not include currency effects.
3. "Others" comprise Korea Development Bank bonds, National Housing bonds, and Seoul Metro bonds.
4. Corporate bonds include equity-linked securities and derivatives-linked securities.
Sources: The Bank of Korea and KG Zeroin Corporation.

Issuance of corporate bonds in the Republic of Korea surged 42.5% q-o-q to KRW171.8 trillion in the fourth quarter of 2021 from KRW120.6 trillion in the previous quarter. The table below lists some of the notable LCY corporate bond issuances in the Republic of Korea during the quarter.

Table 2: Notable Local Currency Corporate Bond Issuances in the Fourth Quarter of 2021

Corporate Issuers	Coupon Rate (%)	Issued Amount (KRW billion)
Industrial Bank of Korea*		
2-month bond		1,880
2-month bond		1,150
3-month bond		610
9-month bond		610
1-year bond	1.28	800
1.5-year bond	1.79	600
1.5-year bond	1.84	510
2-year bond	1.82	510
3-year bond	2.01	700
Shinhan Bank*		
1-year bond	1.58	500
1-year bond	1.41	400
1.5-year bond	1.93	610
1.5-year bond	1.89	600
1.5-year bond	1.89	350
1.5-year bond	1.97	350
1.5-year bond	1.90	300
2-year bond	1.91	350
NongHyup Bank*		
1-year bond	1.58	890
1-year bond	1.61	600
1-year bond	1.59	340
10-year bond	2.85	300

Corporate Issuers	Coupon Rate (%)	Issued Amount (KRW billion)
Woori Bank*		
1-year bond	1.60	450
1-year bond	1.45	440
1-year bond	1.41	250
1.5-year bond	1.89	350
1.5-year bond		
Hana Bank*		
1-year bond	1.40	350
1-year bond	0.54	300
1-year bond	1.44	300
1.5-year bond	1.63	260
2-year bond	0.70	280
2-year bond	1.99	270
Korea Electric Power Corporation*		
1-year bond	1.63	250
5-year bond	2.20	200
7-year bond	2.55	250
7-year bond	2.59	230
7-year bond	2.63	200
7-year bond	2.72	200

KRW = Korean won.
[a] Multiple issuance of the same tenor indicates issuance on different dates.
Source: Based on data from Bloomberg LP.

The aggregate bonds outstanding of the top 30 LCY corporate bond issuers in the Republic of Korea reached KRW990.4 trillion, comprising 59.7% of total corporate bonds outstanding at the end of December. Korea Housing Finance Corporation, a government-related institution providing financial assistance for social housing, remained the single-largest corporate bond issuer with outstanding bonds of KRW151.3 trillion. Industrial Bank of Korea and Korea Investment and Securities followed with total bonds outstanding of KRW77.6 trillion and KRW56.2 trillion, respectively.

Table 3: Top 30 Issuers of Local Currency Corporate Bonds in the Republic of Korea

| | Issuers | Outstanding Amount | | State-Owned | Listed on | | Type of Industry |
		LCY Bonds (KRW billion)	LCY Bonds (USD billion)		KOSPI	KOSDAQ	
1.	Korea Housing Finance Corporation	151,260	127.1	Yes	No	No	Housing Finance
2.	Industrial Bank of Korea	77,600	65.2	Yes	Yes	No	Banking
3.	Korea Investment and Securities	56,225	47.3	No	No	No	Securities
4.	Mirae Asset Securities Co.	54,150	45.5	No	Yes	No	Securities
5.	Hana Financial Investment	51,177	43.0	No	No	No	Securities
6.	KB Securities	49,164	41.3	No	No	No	Securities
7.	Shinhan Investment Corporation	42,647	35.8	No	No	No	Securities
8.	Meritz Securities Co.	38,974	32.8	No	Yes	No	Securities
9.	Korea Electric Power Corporation	34,080	28.6	Yes	Yes	No	Electricity, Energy, and Power
10.	NH Investment & Securities	33,942	28.5	Yes	Yes	No	Securities
11.	Shinhan Bank	32,012	26.9	No	No	No	Banking
12.	Korea Land & Housing Corporation	31,026	26.1	Yes	No	No	Real Estate
13.	Samsung Securities	29,850	25.1	No	Yes	No	Securities
14.	Korea Expressway	26,480	22.3	Yes	No	No	Transport Infrastructure
15.	Woori Bank	24,330	20.4	Yes	Yes	No	Banking
16.	The Export–Import Bank of Korea	23,540	19.8	Yes	No	No	Banking
17.	KEB Hana Bank	22,675	19.1	No	No	No	Banking
18.	Kookmin Bank	21,314	17.9	No	No	No	Banking
19.	NongHyup Bank	20,510	17.2	Yes	No	No	Banking
20.	Korea SMEs and Startups Agency	19,528	16.4	Yes	No	No	SME Development
21.	Korea National Railway	19,440	16.3	Yes	No	No	Transport Infrastructure
22.	Hanwha Investment and Securities	18,327	15.4	No	No	No	Securities
23.	Shinyoung Securities	17,208	14.5	No	Yes	No	Securities
24.	Shinhan Card	16,445	13.8	No	No	No	Credit Card
25.	KB Kookmin Bank Card	14,705	12.4	No	No	No	Consumer Finance
26.	Hyundai Capital Services	14,415	12.1	No	No	No	Consumer Finance
27.	Standard Chartered Bank Korea	13,390	11.3	No	No	No	Banking
28.	NongHyup	13,030	11.0	Yes	No	No	Banking
29.	Samsung Card Co.	12,198	10.3	No	Yes	No	Credit Card
30.	Korea Gas Corporation	10,794	9.1	Yes	Yes	No	Gas Utility
	Total Top 30 LCY Corporate Issuers	990,436	832.4				
	Total LCY Corporate Bonds	1,659,300	1,394.5				
	Top 30 as % of Total LCY Corporate Bonds	59.7%	59.7%				

KOSDAQ = Korean Securities Dealer Automated Quotations, KOSPI = Korea Composite Stock Price Index, KRW = Korean won, LCY = local currency, SMEs = small and medium-sized enterprises, USD = United States dollar.
Notes:
1. Data as of 31 December 2021.
2. State-owned firms are defined as those in which the government has more than a 50% ownership stake.
Sources: *AsianBondsOnline* calculations based on Bloomberg LP and KG Zeroin Corporation.

Malaysia

The local currency (LCY) bond market of Malaysia expanded 1.0% quarter-on-quarter (q-o-q) and 8.2% year-on-year in the fourth quarter (Q4) of 2021, reaching a size of MYR1,736.2 billion (USD416.7 billion) at the end of December. LCY government bonds outstanding increased 1.2% q-o-q, driven by a rise in central government bonds, to reach MYR949.4 billion. LCY corporate bonds outstanding recorded MYR786.8 billion at the end of December on growth of 0.8% q-o-q. The aggregate stock of *sukuk* (Islamic bonds) outstanding at the end of the year totaled MYR1,102.7 billion.

Table 1: Size and Composition of the Local Currency Bond Market in Malaysia

| | Outstanding Amount (billion) | | | | | | Growth Rate (%) | | | |
| | Q4 2020 | | Q3 2021 | | Q4 2021 | | Q4 2020 | | Q4 2021 | |
	MYR	USD	MYR	USD	MYR	USD	q-o-q	y-o-y	q-o-q	y-o-y
Total	1,604	399	1,719	411	1,736	417	1.3	8.0	1.0	8.2
Government	853	212	938	224	949	228	0.5	10.3	1.2	11.4
Central Government Bonds	827	206	914	218	931	224	0.8	12.1	1.9	12.7
of which: *sukuk*	384	95	435	104	441	106	1.7	12.4	1.5	15.0
Central Bank Bills	2	0.5	0	0	0	0	(50.0)	(77.8)	–	(100.0)
of which: *sukuk*	0	0	0	0	0	0	–	(100.0)	–	–
Sukuk Perumahan Kerajaan	24	6	24	6	18	4	0.0	(10.1)	(24.9)	(24.9)
Corporate	752	187	780	186	787	189	2.2	5.6	0.8	4.6
of which: *sukuk*	609	151	638	152	643	154	2.8	7.0	0.9	5.7

( ) = negative, – = not applicable, LCY = local currency, MYR = Malaysian ringgit, q-o-q = quarter-on-quarter, Q3 = third quarter, Q4 = fourth quarter, USD = United States dollar, y-o-y = year-on-year.
Notes:
1. Bloomberg LP end-of-period LCY–USD rate is used.
2. Growth rates are calculated from an LCY base and do not include currency effects.
3. *Sukuk Perumahan Kerajaan* are Islamic bonds issued by the government to refinance funding for housing loans to government employees and to extend new housing loans.
Sources: Bank Negara Malaysia Fully Automated System for Issuing/Tendering and Bloomberg LP.

Issuance of LCY bonds expanded 2.6% q-o-q in Q4 2021, led by 7.6% q-o-q growth in LCY corporate bond issuance, which totaled MYR41.2 billion during the quarter. A 1.3% q-o-q contraction in LCY government bond issuances to MYR47.9 billion slightly offset this growth. During the quarter, government-owned institutions DanaInfra Nasional and CIMB Bank had the largest issuance totals.

Table 2: Notable Local Currency Corporate Bond Issuances in the Fourth Quarter of 2021

Corporate Issuers	Coupon Rate (%)	Issued Amount (MYR billion)		Corporate Issuers	Coupon Rate (%)	Issued Amount (MYR billion)
DanaInfra Nasional[a]				CIMB Bank		
7-year Islamic MTN	3.70	400		3-year MTN	Floating	1,000
7-year Islamic MTN	3.72	300		4-year MTN	Floating	1,000
7-year Islamic MTN	3.68	100		5-year MTN	Floating	1,000
14-year Islamic MTN	4.23	615		10-year *sukuk wakalah*	3.80	100
15-year Islamic MTN	4.34	860		Tenaga Nasional		
15-year Islamic MTN	4.34	450		7-year Islamic MTN	3.92	300
20-year Islamic MTN	4.50	270		10-year Islamic MTN	4.08	300
20-year Islamic MTN	4.51	300		15-year Islamic MTN	4.47	1,200
20-year Islamic MTN	4.48	195		20-year Islamic MTN	4.67	1,200
29-year Islamic MTN	4.57	235				
30-year Islamic MTN	4.70	370				
30-year Islamic MTN	4.70	450				

MTN = medium-term note, MYR = Malaysian ringgit.
Note: *Sukuk wakalah* are Islamic bonds in which the bondholder nominates another person to act on his behalf.
[a] Multiple issuance of the same tenor indicates issuance on different dates.
Source: Based on data from Bloomberg LP.

At the end of December, the top 30 issuers had combined outstanding LCY corporate bonds totaling MYR467.3 billion, or 59.4% of the total LCY corporate bond stock. DanaInfra Nasional topped all issuers in terms of outstanding bonds at the end of 2021, while the finance sector led all sectors.

Table 3: Top 30 Issuers of Local Currency Corporate Bonds in Malaysia

	Issuers	Outstanding Amount		State-Owned	Listed Company	Type of Industry
		LCY Bonds (MYR billion)	LCY Bonds (USD billion)			
1.	DanaInfra Nasional	78.8	18.9	Yes	No	Finance
2.	Prasarana	38.3	9.2	Yes	No	Transport, Storage, and Communications
3.	Lembaga Pembiayaan Perumahan Sektor Awam	37.6	9.0	Yes	No	Property and Real Estate
4.	Cagamas	32.3	7.7	Yes	No	Finance
5.	Project Lebuhraya Usahasama	28.9	6.9	No	No	Transport, Storage, and Communications
6.	Urusharta Jamaah	27.3	6.6	Yes	No	Finance
7.	Perbadanan Tabung Pendidikan Tinggi Nasional	23.1	5.5	Yes	No	Finance
8.	Pengurusan Air	18.7	4.5	Yes	No	Energy, Gas, and Water
9.	CIMB Group Holdings	14.3	3.4	Yes	No	Finance
10.	Maybank Islamic	13.0	3.1	No	Yes	Banking
11.	Malayan Banking	12.5	3.0	No	Yes	Banking
12.	Sarawak Energy	12.0	2.9	Yes	No	Energy, Gas, and Water
13.	Khazanah	11.9	2.9	Yes	No	Finance
14.	Tenaga Nasional	11.6	2.8	No	Yes	Energy, Gas, and Water
15.	CIMB Bank	11.6	2.8	Yes	No	Finance
16.	Danga Capital	10.0	2.4	Yes	No	Finance
17.	Jimah East Power	8.8	2.1	Yes	No	Energy, Gas, and Water
18.	Danum Capital	8.4	2.0	No	No	Finance
19.	Public Bank	6.9	1.7	No	No	Banking
20.	Sapura TMC	6.4	1.5	No	No	Finance
21.	Bank Pembangunan Malaysia	6.0	1.4	Yes	No	Banking
22.	Malaysia Rail Link	5.8	1.4	Yes	No	Construction
23.	YTL Power International	5.8	1.4	No	Yes	Energy, Gas, and Water
24.	Infracap Resources	5.8	1.4	Yes	No	Finance
25.	GOVCO Holdings	5.7	1.4	Yes	No	Finance
26.	Bakun Hydro Power Generation	5.5	1.3	No	No	Energy, Gas, and Water
27.	Turus Pesawat	5.3	1.3	Yes	No	Transport, Storage, and Communications
28.	GENM Capital	5.3	1.3	No	No	Finance
29.	EDRA Energy	5.1	1.2	No	Yes	Energy, Gas, and Water
30.	1Malaysia Development	5.0	1.2	Yes	No	Finance
	Total Top 30 LCY Corporate Issuers	**467.3**	**112.1**			
	Total LCY Corporate Bonds	**786.8**	**188.8**			
	Top 30 as % of Total LCY Corporate Bonds	**59.4%**	**59.4%**			

Notes:
1. Data as of 31 December 2021.
2. State-owned firms are defined as those in which the government has more than a 50% ownership stake.
Source: *AsianBondsOnline* calculations based on Bank Negara Malaysia Fully Automated System for Issuing/Tendering data.

Philippines

The Philippines' local currency (LCY) bond market modestly grew 0.3% quarter-on-quarter (q-o-q) to reach PHP9,786.6 billion (USD191.9 billion) at the end of December 2021. Total government bonds outstanding increased 0.5% q-o-q to PHP8,365.2 billion at the end of the fourth quarter (Q4) of 2021, driven entirely by Treasury bond issuance, while outstanding bonds in other government bond market segments declined. Outstanding corporate bonds fell 1.3% q-o-q to PHP1,421.3 billion due to debt maturities outpacing issuance during the quarter. Year-on-year, the Philippines' total LCY bond stock grew 14.2%. Government bonds comprised 85.5% and corporate bonds comprised 14.5% of the LCY bond market at the end of December.

Table 1: Size and Composition of the Local Currency Bond Market in the Philippines

| | Outstanding Amount (billion) | | | | | | Growth Rate (%) | | | |
| | Q4 2020 | | Q3 2021 | | Q4 2021 | | Q4 2020 | | Q4 2021 | |
	PHP	USD	PHP	USD	PHP	USD	q-o-q	y-o-y	q-o-q	y-o-y
Total	8,568	178	9,762	191	9,787	192	5.3	28.9	0.3	14.2
Government	6,956	145	8,322	163	8,365	164	7.0	35.3	0.5	20.3
Treasury Bills	949	20	943	18	796	16	8.3	95.3	(15.5)	(16.1)
Treasury Bonds	5,720	119	6,880	135	7,267	143	3.3	23.9	5.6	27.0
Central Bank Securities	220	5	440	9	260	5	340.0	–	(40.9)	18.2
Others	66	1	60	1	42	1	65.3	65.2	(30.3)	(36.7)
Corporate	1,612	34	1,440	28	1,421	28	(1.3)	7.1	(1.3)	(11.8)

( ) = negative, – = not applicable, LCY = local currency, PHP = Philippine peso, q-o-q = quarter-on-quarter, Q3 = third quarter, Q4 = fourth quarter, USD = United States dollar, y-o-y = year-on-year.
Notes:
1. Bloomberg end-of-period LCY–USD rates are used.
2. Growth rates are calculated from an LCY base and do not include currency effects.
3. "Others" comprise bonds issued by government agencies, entities, and corporations for which repayment is guaranteed by the Government of the Philippines. This includes bonds issued by Power Sector Assets and Liabilities Management (PSALM) and the National Food Authority, among others.
4. Peso Global Bonds (PHP-denominated bonds payable in US dollars) are not included.
Sources: Bloomberg LP and Bureau of the Treasury.

Corporate bond issuance increased 18.4% q-o-q in Q4 2021, totaling PHP58.5 billion. The table below lists all debt sales during the quarter, comprising 11 bond issuances from eight firms. SM Prime Holding had the single-largest issuance of PHP 10.0 billion.

Table 2: Notable Local Currency Corporate Bond Issuances in the Fourth Quarter of 2021

Corporate Issuers	Coupon Rate (%)	Issued Amount (PHP billion)	Corporate Issuers	Coupon Rate (%)	Issued Amount (PHP billion)
SM Prime Holdings			Ayala Land		
7-year bond	5.10	10.00	10-year bond	4.08	3.00
Petron			AREIT, Inc.		
4-year bond	3.44	9.00	2-year bond	3.04	3.00
6-year bond	4.34	9.00	SL Agritech		
Aboitiz Power			1-year bond	zero coupon	1.87
4-year bond	4.00	4.80	Alsons Consolidated Resources		
7-year bond	5.03	7.20	1-year bond	zero coupon	0.60
Filinvest Land					
4-year bond	4.50	5.00			
6-year bond	5.26	5.00			

PHP = Philippine peso.
Source: Based on data from Bloomberg LP.

The aggregate amount of LCY bonds outstanding of the top 30 corporate issuers amounted to PHP1,274.7 billion at the end of December, representing 89.7% of the entire LCY corporate bond market. Banks continued to hold the largest sectoral share in the corporate bond market at 40.9%, followed by holding firms (24.0%) and property firms (17.4%). BDO Unibank and SM Prime Holdings were the largest LCY corporate bond issuers at the end of Q4 2021, with outstanding debt of over PHP100.0 billion each.

Table 3: Top 30 Issuers of Local Currency Corporate Bonds in the Philippines

	Issuers	Outstanding Amount		State-Owned	Listed Company	Type of Industry
		LCY Bonds (PHP billion)	LCY Bonds (USD billion)			
1.	BDO Unibank	109.9	2.2	No	Yes	Banking
2.	SM Prime Holdings	103.3	2.0	No	Yes	Holding Firms
3.	Ayala Land	95.9	1.9	No	Yes	Property
4.	Metropolitan Bank	93.8	1.8	No	Yes	Banking
5.	San Miguel	90.0	1.8	No	Yes	Holding Firms
6.	SMC Global Power	73.8	1.4	No	No	Electricity, Energy, and Power
7.	Bank of the Philippine Islands	61.8	1.2	No	Yes	Banking
8.	China Bank	61.2	1.2	No	Yes	Banking
9.	Rizal Commercial Banking Corporation	55.1	1.1	No	Yes	Banking
10.	Aboitiz Power	50.0	1.0	No	Yes	Electricity, Energy, and Power
11.	Security Bank	48.3	0.9	No	Yes	Banking
12.	Petron	45.0	0.9	No	Yes	Electricity, Energy, and Power
13.	Vista Land	42.7	0.8	No	Yes	Property
14.	Ayala Corporation	40.0	0.8	No	Yes	Holding Firms
15.	Philippine National Bank	31.8	0.6	No	Yes	Banking
16.	Filinvest Land	30.5	0.6	No	Yes	Property
17.	Aboitiz Equity Ventures	27.6	0.5	No	Yes	Holding Firms
18.	Robinsons Land	25.2	0.5	No	Yes	Property
19.	Union Bank of the Philippines	24.6	0.5	No	Yes	Banking
20.	SM Investments	23.3	0.5	No	Yes	Holding Firms
21.	Philippine Savings Bank	19.1	0.4	No	Yes	Banking
22.	Maynilad	18.5	0.4	No	No	Water
23.	East West Banking	16.2	0.3	No	Yes	Banking
24.	Doubledragon	15.0	0.3	No	Yes	Property
25.	San Miguel Food and Beverage	15.0	0.3	No	Yes	Food and Beverage
26.	Megaworld	12.0	0.2	No	Yes	Property
27.	Puregold	12.0	0.2	No	Yes	Whole and Retail Trading
28.	MTD Manila Expressway	11.5	0.2	No	No	Infrastructure
29.	Metro Pacific Investments	11.4	0.2	No	Yes	Holding Firms
30.	GT Capital	10.1	0.2	No	Yes	Holding Firms
	Total Top 30 LCY Corporate Issuers	**1,274.7**	**25.0**			
	Total LCY Corporate Bonds	**1,421.3**	**27.9**			
	Top 30 as % of Total LCY Corporate Bonds	**89.7%**	**89.7%**			

LCY = local currency, PHP = Philippine peso, USD = United States dollar.
Notes:
1. Data as of 31 December 2021.
2. State-owned firms are defined as those in which the government has more than a 50% ownership stake.
Source: *AsianBondsOnline* calculations based on Bloomberg LP data.

Singapore

The local currency (LCY) bond market of Singapore grew 3.8% quarter-on-quarter (q-o-q) and 21.9% year-on-year in the fourth quarter (Q4) of 2021, with total bonds outstanding of SGD606.3 billion (USD449.5 billion) at the end of December. LCY government bonds increased 4.1% q-o-q to SGD411.5 billion, led by Monetary Authority of Singapore bills. LCY corporate bonds outstanding reached SGD194.8 billion at the end of the review period on growth of 3.3% q-o-q.

Table 1: Size and Composition of the Local Currency Bond Market in Singapore

| | Outstanding Amount (billion) | | | | | | Growth Rate (%) | | | |
| | Q4 2020 | | Q3 2021 | | Q4 2021 | | Q4 2020 | | Q4 2021 | |
	SGD	USD	SGD	USD	SGD	USD	q-o-q	y-o-y	q-o-q	y-o-y
Total	498	376	584	430	606	449	3.6	10.4	3.8	21.9
Government	330	249	395	291	412	305	5.3	15.3	4.1	24.9
SGS Bills and Bonds	196	148	216	159	214	159	2.6	7.4	(0.6)	9.2
MAS Bills	133	101	180	132	197	146	9.4	29.3	9.7	48.0
Corporate	168	127	189	139	195	144	0.5	1.8	3.3	16.0

( ) = negative, LCY = local currency, MAS = Monetary Authority of Singapore, q-o-q = quarter-on-quarter, Q3 = third quarter, Q4 = fourth quarter, SGD = Singapore dollar, SGS = Singapore Government Securities, USD = United States dollar, y-o-y = year-on-year.
Notes:
1. Corporate bonds are based on *AsianBondsOnline* estimates.
2. SGS bills and bonds do not include the special issue of SGS held by the Singapore Central Provident Fund.
3. Bloomberg LP end-of-period LCY–USD rates are used.
4. Growth rates are calculated from an LCY base and do not include currency effects.
Sources: Bloomberg LP, Monetary Authority of Singapore, and Singapore Government Securities.

LCY bond issuance during the quarter expanded 18.0% q-o-q in Q4 2021 as government bond issuance jumped 19.0% q-o-q to SGD323.2 billion. The contraction in LCY corporate bond issuance of 18.6% q-o-q to SGD5.9 billion slightly offset this growth. During the review period, the largest issuances came from the Housing & Development Board and the Singapore Institute of Technology.

Table 2: Notable Local Currency Corporate Bond Issuances in the Fourth Quarter of 2021

Corporate Issuers	Coupon Rate (%)	Issued Amount (SGD million)
Housing & Development Board		
5-year bond	1.65	1,000
7-year bond	1.54	900
Singapore Institute of Technology		
Perpetual bond	Floating	500
Mapletree Logistics Trust		
Perpetual bond	Floating	400
Tuan Sing Holdings		
3-year bond	6.90	200
Cromwell European Real Estate Investment Trust		
Perpetual bond	Floating	100

SGD = Singapore dollar.
Source: Bloomberg LP.

The top 30 issuers of corporate bonds at the end of December had combined LCY corporate bonds outstanding of SGD106.8 billion, or 54.8% of the total LCY corporate bond stock. The government-owned Housing & Development Board topped all issuers in terms of outstanding corporate bonds at the end 2021, while the real estate sector topped all sectors.

Table 3: Top 30 Issuers of Local Currency Corporate Bonds in Singapore

	Issuers	Outstanding Amount		State-Owned	Listed Company	Type of Industry
		LCY Bonds (SGD billion)	LCY Bonds (USD billion)			
1.	Housing & Development Board	25.9	19.2	Yes	No	Real Estate
2.	Singapore Airlines	14.7	10.9	Yes	Yes	Transportation
3.	Land Transport Authority	9.5	7.0	Yes	No	Transportation
4.	CapitaLand	5.6	4.1	Yes	Yes	Real Estate
5.	Temasek Financial	5.1	3.8	Yes	No	Finance
6.	United Overseas Bank	4.0	3.0	No	Yes	Banking
7.	Frasers Property	3.8	2.8	No	Yes	Real Estate
8.	Sembcorp Industries	3.8	2.8	No	Yes	Diversified
9.	Mapletree Treasury Services	3.3	2.4	No	No	Finance
10.	DBS Bank	2.9	2.1	No	Yes	Banking
11.	Keppel Corporation	2.6	1.9	No	Yes	Diversified
12.	City Developments Limited	2.1	1.5	No	Yes	Real Estate
13.	CapitaLand Mall Trust	2.0	1.5	No	No	Finance
14.	Olam International	2.0	1.5	No	Yes	Consumer Goods
15.	Oversea-Chinese Banking Corporation	1.7	1.3	No	Yes	Banking
16.	Singapore Technologies Telemedia	1.7	1.2	Yes	No	Utilities
17.	National Environment Agency	1.7	1.2	Yes	No	Environmental Services
18.	Shangri-La Hotel	1.5	1.1	No	Yes	Real Estate
19.	Ascendas Real Estate Investment Trust	1.5	1.1	No	Yes	Finance
20.	NTUC Income	1.4	1.0	No	No	Finance
21.	GuocoLand Limited IHT	1.4	1.0	No	No	Real Estate
22.	Singtel Group Treasury	1.3	0.9	No	No	Finance
23.	Suntec Real Estate Investment Trust	1.2	0.9	No	Yes	Real Estate
24.	Public Utilities Board	1.0	0.7	Yes	No	Utilities
25.	Ascott Residence	1.0	0.7	No	Yes	Real Estate
26.	Singapore Press Holdings	1.0	0.7	No	Yes	Communications
27.	Keppel Real Estate Investment Trust	0.9	0.7	No	No	Real Estate
28.	StarHub	0.9	0.7	No	Yes	Diversified
29.	Keppel Land International	0.9	0.7	No	No	Real Estate
30.	Hyflux	0.9	0.7	No	Yes	Utilities
	Total Top 30 LCY Corporate Issuers	**106.8**	**79.2**			
	Total LCY Corporate Bonds	**194.8**	**144.4**			
	Top 30 as % of Total LCY Corporate Bonds	**54.8%**	**54.8%**			

LCY = local currency, SGD = Singapore dollar, USD = United States dollar.
Notes:
1. Data as of 31 December 2021.
2. State-owned firms are defined as those in which the government has more than a 50% ownership stake.
Source: *AsianBondsOnline* calculations based on Bloomberg LP data.

Thailand

Total local currency (LCY) bonds outstanding in Thailand amounted to THB14.7 trillion (USD443.5 billion) at the end of the fourth quarter (Q4) of 2021. Overall growth eased to 1.1% quarter-on-quarter (q-o-q) in Q4 2021 from 2.5% q-o-q in the third (Q3) quarter, driven by weaker growth in both the government and corporate bond segments. Government bonds outstanding rose 1.6% q-o-q in Q4 2021, down from 2.2% q-o-q in the previous quarter. The corporate bond segment posted marginal growth of 0.01% in Q4 2021 versus 3.4% q-o-q in Q3 2021.

Table 1: Size and Composition of the Local Currency Bond Market in Thailand

| | Outstanding Amount (billion) | | | | | | Growth Rate (%) | | | |
| | Q4 2020 | | Q3 2021 | | Q4 2021 | | Q4 2020 | | Q4 2021 | |
	THB	USD	THB	USD	THB	USD	q-o-q	y-o-y	q-o-q	y-o-y
Total	13,923	465	14,563	432	14,728	443	(0.7)	5.2	1.1	5.8
Government	10,232	342	10,552	313	10,716	323	(0.3)	8.3	1.6	4.7
Government Bonds and Treasury Bills	6,020	201	6,683	198	6,883	207	5.0	21.9	3.0	14.3
Central Bank Bonds	3,365	112	2,926	87	2,898	87	(9.1)	(9.5)	(1.0)	(13.9)
State-Owned Enterprise and Other Bonds	846	28	943	28	936	28	2.8	6.7	(0.7)	10.6
Corporate	3,692	123	4,011	119	4,011	121	(1.8)	(2.5)	0.01	8.6

( ) = negative, LCY = local currency, q-o-q = quarter-on-quarter, Q3 = third quarter, Q4 = fourth quarter, THB = Thai baht, USD = United States dollar, y-o-y = year-on-year.
Notes:
1. Bloomberg end-of-period LCY–USD rates are used.
2. Growth rates are calculated from an LCY base and do not include currency effects.
Source: Bank of Thailand.

New issuance of corporate bonds totaled THB366.7 billion in Q4 2021, down from THB470.5 billion in Q3 2021. The contraction in issuance deepened, accelerating to 22.1% q-o-q in Q4 2021 from 1.4% q-o-q in the previous quarter, as uncertainties brought about by the prolonged pandemic continued to dampen investor confidence. True Corporation led all issuers of new corporate debt during the quarter, with its total issuance reaching THB30.0 billion.

Table 2: Notable Local Currency Corporate Bond Issuances in the Fourth Quarter of 2021

Corporate Issuers	Coupon Rate (%)	Issued Amount (THB billion)	Corporate Issuers	Coupon Rate (%)	Issued Amount (THB billion)
True Corporation			Bangkok Mass Transit System		
1.2-year bond	0.00	2.0	3-year bond	2.00	2.0
1.3-year bond	0.00	3.0	5-year bond	2.70	1.5
1.4-year bond	0.00	1.0	7-year bond	3.12	2.5
2-year bond	2.75	1.5	10-year bond	3.66	4.2
3-year bond	3.20	6.2	Indorama Ventures		
4-year bond	3.60	4.2	5-year bond	2.48	3.0
5-year bond	4.05	4.9	7-year bond	3.00	2.0
7-year bond	4.60	7.2	10.5-year bond	3.60	5.0
Siam Cement			CP ALL		
4-year bond	2.65	25.0	Perpetual bond	4.60	10.0
Ayudhya Capital					
2-year bond	1.13	1.3			
10-year bond	3.00	10.0			

THB = Thai baht.
Source: Bloomberg LP.

The aggregate LCY bonds outstanding of the top 30 corporate issuers in Thailand amounted to THB2,358.8 billion at the end of Q4 2021, comprising a 58.8% share of the total LCY corporate bond market. CP ALL was the top issuer, with total outstanding LCY bonds of THB252.5 billion at the end of December. Food and beverage firms held the largest share of outstanding corporate bonds among all sectors, amounting to a combined THB383.3 billion.

Table 3: Top 30 Issuers of Local Currency Corporate Bonds in Thailand

	Issuers	Outstanding Amount		State-Owned	Listed Company	Type of Industry
		LCY Bonds (THB billion)	LCY Bonds (USD billion)			
1.	CP ALL	252.5	7.6	No	Yes	Commerce
2.	Thai Beverage	173.1	5.2	No	No	Food and Beverage
3.	Siam Cement	165.0	5.0	Yes	Yes	Construction Material
4.	True Corporation	160.9	4.8	No	No	Communications
5.	Charoen Pokphand Foods	131.2	4.0	No	Yes	Food and Beverage
6.	PTT	124.4	3.7	Yes	Yes	Energy and Utilities
7.	Berli Jucker	109.6	3.3	No	Yes	Commerce
8.	Bank of Ayudhya	97.8	2.9	No	Yes	Banking
9.	True Move H Universal Communication	88.1	2.7	No	No	Communication
10.	CPF Thailand	79.1	2.4	No	No	Food and Beverage
11.	Indorama Ventures	73.0	2.2	No	Yes	Petrochemicals and Chemicals
12.	Minor International	67.8	2.0	No	Yes	Hospitality and Leisure
13.	Toyota Leasing Thailand	67.6	2.0	No	No	Finance and Securities
14.	Bangkok Commercial Asset Management	62.2	1.9	No	Yes	Finance and Securities
15.	Banpu	61.3	1.8	No	Yes	Energy and Utilities
16.	Frasers Property Thailand	49.3	1.5	No	Yes	Property and Construction
17.	TPI Polene	47.5	1.4	No	Yes	Property and Construction
18.	Gulf Energy Development	47.5	1.4	No	Yes	Energy and Utilities
19.	Muangthai Capital	47.2	1.4	No	Yes	Finance and Securities
20.	BTS Group Holdings	45.1	1.4	No	Yes	Diversified
21.	Krungthai Card	44.5	1.3	Yes	Yes	Banking
22.	Krung Thai Bank	44.0	1.3	Yes	Yes	Banking
23.	dtac TriNet	43.5	1.3	No	Yes	Communications
24.	Global Power Synergy	41.5	1.2	No	Yes	Energy and Utilies
25.	Bangchak	40.5	1.2	No	Yes	Energy and Utilities
26.	Bangkok Expressway & Metro	40.1	1.2	No	Yes	Transportation and Logistics
27.	ICBC Thai Leasing	39.0	1.2	No	No	Finance and Securities
28.	Sansiri	38.8	1.2	No	Yes	Property and Construction
29.	Land & Houses	38.6	1.2	No	Yes	Property and Construction
30.	CH Karnchang	38.4	1.2	No	Yes	Property and Construction
	Total Top 30 LCY Corporate Issuers	2,358.8	71.0			
	Total LCY Corporate Bonds	4,011.2	120.8			
	Top 30 as % of Total LCY Corporate Bonds	58.8%	58.8%			

LCY = local currency, THB = Thai baht, USD = United States dollar.
Notes:
1. Data as of 31 December 2021.
2. State-owned firms are defined as those in which the government has more than a 50% ownership stake.
Source: *AsianBondsOnline* calculations based on Bloomberg LP data.

Viet Nam

Viet Nam's local currency (LCY) bond market grew 9.8% quarter-on-quarter (q-o-q) to reach VND2,089.1 trillion (USD91.5 billion) at the end of December. On an annual basis, the market expanded 25.5%. The quarterly growth was driven by both government and corporate bonds, with outstanding bonds in these segments increasing 5.3% q-o-q and 22.7% q-o-q, respectively, which in both cases was a faster growth rate than in the previous quarter. Outstanding government bonds and corporate bonds comprised 71.3% and 28.7% of the LCY bond market, respectively, at the end of December 2021.

Table 1: Size and Composition of the Local Currency Bond Market in Viet Nam

	Outstanding Amount (billion)						Growth Rate (%)			
	Q4 2020		Q3 2021		Q4 2021		Q4 2020		Q4 2021	
	VND	USD	VND	USD	VND	USD	q-o-q	y-o-y	q-o-q	y-o-y
Total	1,664,554	72	1,903,088	84	2,089,053	92	8.1	31.4	9.8	25.5
Government	1,379,079	60	1,414,481	62	1,489,606	65	7.0	18.7	5.3	8.0
Treasury Bonds	1,227,742	53	1,276,988	56	1,349,811	59	6.8	22.8	5.7	9.9
Central Bank Bonds	0	0	0	0	0	0	–	–	–	–
State-Owned Enterprise Bonds	151,337	7	137,494	6	139,796	6	8.1	(6.8)	1.7	(7.6)
Corporate	285,475	12	488,607	21	599,446	26	13.9	172.4	22.7	110.0

( ) = negative, – = not applicable, LCY = local currency, q-o-q = quarter-on-quarter, Q3 = third quarter, Q4 = fourth quarter, USD = United States dollar, VND = Vietnamese dong, y-o-y = year-on-year.
Notes:
1. Bloomberg LP end-of-period LCY–USD rates are used.
2. Growth rates are calculated from an LCY base and do not include currency effects.
Sources: Bloomberg LP and Vietnam Bond Market Association.

Corporate bond issuance in Viet Nam jumped 30.8% q-o-q in the fourth quarter (Q4) of 2021 to VND123.4 trillion as more firms turned to the bond market to raise funds. The table below lists notable bond sales during the quarter, led by Thai Son-Long An JSC with a single VND4.6 trillion issuance. The largest debt issuers in Q4 2021 were mainly from the property sector.

Table 2: Local Currency Corporate Bond Issuances in the Fourth Quarter of 2021

Corporate Issuer	Coupon Rate (%)	Issued Amount (VND billion)
Thai Son - Long An JSC		
8-year bond	Variable coupon	4,600
Osaka Garden Corporation		
2-year bond	Variable coupon	4,300
Sunvalley Invest JSC		
4-year bond	–	3,560
Bach Hung Vuong JSC		
1-year bond	–	2,980
Wealth Power JSC		
1-year bond	–	2,880
S-Vin Real Estate JSC		
3-year bond	Variable coupon	2,500
Vietnam Prosperity Joint Stock Commercial Bank[a]		
3-year bond	2.40	2,500
3-year bond	2.40	2,500

– = not available, JSC = Joint Stock Corporation, VND = Vietnamese dong.
[a] Multiple issuance of the same tenor indicates issuance on different dates.
Source: Vietnam Bond Market Association.

The top 30 corporate issuers had aggregate LCY bonds outstanding of VND358.7 trillion at the end of December, accounting for 59.8% of the total LCY corporate bond market. About 75% of the top 30's debt stock was issued by banks, totaling VND275.4 trillion, while property firms had the second-highest share at 13.2% (VND47.3 trillion). All firms with more than VND10.0 trillion of outstanding bonds were from the banking sector except for the Masan Group. The Bank for Investment and Development of Vietnam was the largest issuer among the top 30 list with total bonds outstanding of VND37.2 trillion at the end of Q4 2021.

Table 3: Top 30 Issuers of Local Currency Corporate Bonds in Viet Nam

	Issuers	Outstanding Amount LCY Bonds (VND billion)	Outstanding Amount LCY Bonds (USD billion)	State-Owned	Listed Company	Type of Industry
1.	Bank for Investment and Development of Vietnam	37,240	1.63	Yes	Yes	Banking
2.	Vietnam Prosperity Joint Stock Commercial Bank	29,050	1.27	No	Yes	Banking
3.	Ho Chi Minh City Development Joint Stock Commercial Bank	28,768	1.26	No	Yes	Banking
4.	Vietnam International Joint Stock Commercial Bank	26,950	1.18	No	Yes	Banking
5.	Lien Viet Post Joint Stock Commercial Bank	24,090	1.06	No	Yes	Banking
6.	Asia Commercial Joint Stock Bank	21,900	0.96	No	Yes	Banking
7.	Orient Commercial Joint Stock Bank	18,535	0.81	No	No	Banking
8.	Tien Phong Commercial Joint Stock Bank	17,649	0.77	No	Yes	Banking
9.	Masan Group	16,900	0.74	No	Yes	Finance
10.	Vietnam Joint Stock Commercial Bank for Industry and Trade	13,389	0.59	Yes	Yes	Banking
11.	Saigon - Ha Noi Commercial Joint Stock Bank	11,250	0.49	No	Yes	Banking
12.	An Binh Commercial Joint Stock Bank	10,500	0.46	No	No	Banking
13.	Vietnam Maritime Joint Stock Commercial Bank	8,999	0.39	No	Yes	Banking
14.	Sovico Group Joint Stock Company	8,550	0.37	No	Yes	Property
15.	Saigon Glory Company Limited	8,000	0.35	No	No	Property
16.	Bac A Commercial Joint Stock Bank	6,140	0.27	No	Yes	Banking
17.	Southeast Asia Commercial Joint Stock Bank	6,077	0.27	No	Yes	Banking
18.	Golden Hill Real Estate JSC	5,701	0.25	No	No	Property
19.	Vinhomes Joint Stock Company	5,565	0.24	No	Yes	Property
20.	Vingroup	5,425	0.24	No	Yes	Property
21.	Ho Chi Minh City Infrastructure Investment Joint Stock Company	5,370	0.24	No	Yes	Construction
22.	Military Commercial Joint Stock Bank	5,216	0.23	No	Yes	Banking
23.	Mediterranean Revival Villas Company Limited	5,000	0.22	No	No	Property
24.	Vietnam Technological and Commercial Joint Stock Bank	5,000	0.22	No	Yes	Banking
25.	Bong Sen JSC	4,800	0.21	No	No	Manufacturing
26.	Thai Son - Long An JSC	4,600	0.20	No	No	Property
27.	Vietnam Bank for Agriculture and Rural Development	4,600	0.20	Yes	No	Banking
28.	Trung Nam Dak Lak 1 Wind Power JSC	4,500	0.20	No	No	Energy
29.	Phu My Hung Corporation	4,497	0.20	No	No	Property
30.	Truong Hai Auto Corporation	4,400	0.19	No	No	Manufacturing
	Total Top 30 LCY Corporate Issuers	358,660	15.71			
	Total LCY Corporate Bonds	599,446	26.26			
	Top 31 as % of Total LCY Corporate Bonds	59.8%	59.8%			

LCY = local currency, USD = United States dollar, VND = Vietnamese dong.
Notes:
1. Data as of 31 December 2021.
2. State-owned firms are defined as those in which the government has more than a 50% ownership stake.
Source: *AsianBondsOnline* calculations based on Bloomberg LP data.

CPSIA information can be obtained
at www.ICGtesting.com
Printed in the USA
LVHW070723280622
722266LV00009B/81

9 789292 694265